on track ...

The Sensational Alex Harvey Band

every album, every song

Peter Gallagher

sonicbondpublishing.com

Sonicbond Publishing Limited
www.sonicbondpublishing.co.uk
Email: info@sonicbondpublishing.co.uk

First Published in the United Kingdom 2023
First Published in the United States 2023

British Library Cataloguing in Publication Data:
A Catalogue record for this book is available from the British Library

Copyright Peter Gallagher 2023

ISBN 978-1-78952-289-1

Typeset in ITC Garamond Std & ITC Avant Garde Gothic
Printed and bound in England

Graphic design and typesetting: Full Moon Media

Follow us on social media:
Twitter: https://twitter.com/SonicbondP
Instagram: www.instagram.com/sonicbondpublishing_/
Facebook: www.facebook.com/SonicbondPublishing/

Linktree QR code:

Many thanks to:
James Hamilton, for getting the ball rolling.
Joe Black, for running with it.
and
Zal Cleminson, Janet Macoska, and Owen Mullen,
for their time and their memories.

on track ...

The Sensational Alex Harvey Band

Contents

Introduction: Vambo, and How He Came Into The World

I am a man which am a Jew of Tarsus, a city in Cilicia, a citizen of no mean
city, and I beseech thee, suffer me to speak unto the people.
St. Paul, Acts 21:39

When Saint Paul spoke of his hometown, he didn't use the word 'mean' to
indicate cruel or unpleasant, but rather lowly or of poor quality. In other
words, by stating Tarsus was 'no mean city' he was saying that it was a town of
significance and importance. When the phrase was later applied to Glasgow,
however, it became a byword meaning precisely cruel and unpleasant, thanks
to the novel *No Mean City* by Alexander McArthur and H. Kingsley Long.
Published in 1935, the year Alex Harvey was born, it presents the Gorbals, the
area Harvey largely grew up in, as a bleak, slum-ridden, densely populated
landscape of unrelenting poverty and violence, the latter personified by the
book's protagonist, the self-styled 'razor king', Johnnie Stark.

The book was quickly dismissed by the city fathers and the media as
inaccurate and sensationalist, but they were concerned more about the novel's
potential negative impact on Glasgow's reputation than its accuracy. *No Mean
City* had its moments of melodrama, but it was more social realism than
penny dreadful. The Great Depression had hit Glasgow much as it had the
rest of Europe and North America, resulting in mass unemployment, while
chronic overcrowding and poor sanitation in areas such as the Gorbals meant
disease and death were commonplace, while malnutrition, alcohol addiction,
domestic abuse and sectarian violence were all on a sickening rise. According
to David Montgomery, in his dissertation on the Sensational Alex Harvey
Band song 'The Tomahawk Kid', the Gorbals was 'the only ghetto in the
United Kingdom at that time which might have rivalled those in New York,
Chicago, or Detroit in terms of squalor and violence'. This, then, was the
environment Alex Harvey was born into, on 4 February 1935.

Or was it? Harvey's birthplace seems to shift depending on whoever is
writing about him. In a 2019 article on the singer in the Glasgow *Evening
Times* newspaper, Kinning Park, which lies to the west of the Gorbals, was
identified as Harvey's birthplace, and one would hope professional reporters
would get their facts right. Kinning Park is also a popular online option. The
April 2000 issue of *Mojo* magazine, meanwhile, goes further west and settles
on Govan. We will allow the article's writer the benefit of the doubt; perhaps
he was getting mixed up with Govan Road, part of which is in the Gorbals,
and is the location biographer John Neil Munro plumps for in his book *The
Sensational Alex Harvey*. This is also identified as Harvey's birthplace in the
book, written by Tim Barr, that formed part of *Alex Harvey: The Last of the
Teenage Idols*, an extensive fourteen-disc career retrospective box set released
by Universal Music in 2016. With these two stalwarts rooting for it, it seems

Govan Road is the safe bet, although the Harvey family – father Leslie, mother Greta, and baby Alex – soon relocated to Thistle Street, also in the Gorbals.

It was to Thistle Street that Harvey returned in 1975, out to revisit his past in the company of *Melody Maker*'s Allan Jones. Some of his memories are charming, as he recalled a woman that owned a goat, or singing 'My Cup Runneth Over' at the Sunday school on the corner. It all sounds very endearing, very *Little House on the Prairie*, and not at all Gorbals grim. That soon changes.

'There were hundreds of people lived in this street', he tells Jones, 'and there were lines of demarcation. If you didn't live here, you weren't welcome. It was our territory, and you didnae fuck wi' us'.

'See this wall? There used to be a bullet hole … Aye, fuck, it's still fucking there. Will ye look at that?'

'We used to drop bread into it, that horrible fucking hole, and the rats would come out for the bread, and we'd drop bricks on the little bastards and squash them tae fuck'.

'Some kids got two police dogs, cut their heads off and pinned them to the wall with bayonets'.

Later, in a bar, one of Harvey's old pals recalls a man being attacked with hammers, knives, and hatchets. 'They completely destroyed him', concludes the friend. 'It was the most terrible thing I have ever seen'. Jones reports Harvey nodding in grave agreement.

Maybe not so bucolic, then. The canine cops story sounds a bit suspect, and no amount of rummaging through old newspapers at Glasgow's Mitchell Library shed any light on such an incident. Perhaps it was just an urban myth; this was the land of the Gorbals Vampire after all, a famous case of mass hysteria in 1954 that saw hundreds of local children arm themselves with homemade weapons and descend upon the Southern Necropolis to kill a monster with iron teeth that had devoured two local kids. Like the decapitated dogs, no children had been reported missing, let alone eaten, but it is tempting to think that Alex's then ten-year-old brother Leslie Jnr. might have been amongst the prepubescent vampire hunters. It is also worth remembering that the teller of this shaggy dog story would regularly claim to have been an apprentice lion tamer, a trade that Glasgow, like every other city on the planet, hadn't much call for.

Tall tales aside, the Gorbals of the 1930s, '40s, and '50s was a grim soot-stained landscape of violence, poverty, and desolation, and Glasgow was indeed a mean city, an environment in which the young Alex soon learned how to take care of himself. Despite this, Harvey remembered his childhood fondly. Talking in 1974 on a promotional interview disc sent out to US radio stations, he said:

As far as I am concerned, I had a great childhood. Although it was a tough place to live, and it was wild, there was warmth. Where I lived at that particular time, you didn't have to lock your door at all, because that was your part of the street, and you knew everybody else and no one would steal from the man next door. We had a communal toilet, about 100 people used it, so that brings about a certain amount of togetherness, I suppose.

It didn't hurt that there were certain points of light that helped dispel the darkness, and these would impact every bit as much on Harvey as the harshness of his surroundings. Despite his oldest son having left Strathbungo senior secondary school in 1950 with no formal qualifications, Leslie Snr. believed education was his children's best path of breaking free of the Gorbals and its poverty. He didn't want his sons believing their only opportunities lay in following the accepted path for working-class men in Glasgow, which was to get a job in the shipyards or the docks. Instead, he encouraged his children to think big, and to expand their knowledge by reading everything and anything. For Alex, who soon became a voracious and lifelong reader, the printed page became an escape route out of the drudgery of Gorbals life. He enjoyed history (speciality: the British Empire), which he saw not as some dusty subject on the school curriculum but as a library containing several millennia worth of stories, and also classics by writers such as Robert Louis Stevenson and James Fenimore Cooper, which in turn led to a love of 'boys own' adventure-style stories, science fiction, and comic books.

Cinema, or the 'flicks', was another way in which the young Harvey was able to step outside of the now. Glasgow was the cinema capital of the world back then, boasting over 110 picture houses, more per head than any other city in the world, all providing much-needed escapism during the Depression years and the misery of the Second World War. The country's biggest cinema was Green's Playhouse in Renfield Street, which opened in 1927 with a capacity of more than 4,000. As the Glasgow Apollo, it would later host some of the Sensational Alex Harvey Band's most memorable gigs.

Harvey became an avid cinemagoer, as he recalled to rock photographer Janet Macoska in 1974. 'When I was 15 and I lived in the Gorbals, the only thing you could do – there was no television then – the only escape really was the movies. During the war, I went as many times as I could steal the money, or get into the pictures for nothing, to see anything that was a big Hollywood spectacular; from cowboys to monster movies. I loved entertainers like Fred Astaire'. He would later tell music journalist Charles Shaar Murray that *King Kong* 'was the greatest film ever made'. At the time he was speaking, in the mid-1970s, many might agree; his assertion that the Eighth Wonder of the World was also 'the very first rock and roll hero' is less convincing.

Music was the third light piercing the Glasgow gloom. As with cinemas, the city punched above its weight when it came to dancehalls, boasting more than any other in the United Kingdom, including London. Once legendary venues such as the Locarno, the Plaza, and the colossal Dennistoun Palais may now linger only in the memories of a dwindling generation, but others

9

maintain a spectral presence. The Barrowland Ballroom, for example, is not a ballroom but a concert venue; however, it *did* begin as a dancehall and even outlived most of the competition, surviving into the early 1970s before changing tastes and possible guilt by association with serial killer Bible John sealed its fate. After flirting with roller disco in the late '70s, it reopened as a live music venue in 1983 but much of its décor and design remains as it was in its dancehall days, from the gigantic neon sign emblazoned on the front of the building to the acoustic ceiling tiles installed at the request of band leader Billy McGregor, whose band The Gaybirds foxtrotted and waltzed thirty-six years' worth of Glasgow couples at the venue. The Astoria was another legendary name, now expired, but which enjoys an afterlife as the Garage nightclub and venue on Sauchiehall Street.

'The Dancin'', as it became universally known, was an unchanging aspect of Glasgow culture from the 1930s through to the 1960s, but big band music did not go unchallenged. Dixieland jazz became increasingly popular from the 1930s on, with legends such as Jelly Roll Morton and Louis Armstrong's Hot Five enjoying radio success and jazz clubs springing up around the city. Artists such as Jimmie Rodgers, Roy Acuff and Gene Autry sparked a pre-World War Two interest in 'cowboy music', and the likes of Hank Williams and Red Foley kept the campfire burning into the atomic age. Meanwhile, those in the know were becoming aware of the electric blues of Muddy Waters, Willie Dixon, and Big Bill Broonzy.

One of those in the know was young Alex Harvey, who, unusually for a teenager, then and now, recognised the strengths and validity of all music genres, which would be reflected in the eclecticism of his later recording career. For now, though, Harvey was taking baby steps, jazz having encouraged him to take up the trumpet, take lessons, and play in bands across the city, primarily the Kinning Park Ramblers. The arrival of country and blues, however, plus the generosity of an uncle who noticed his nephew's burgeoning interest in popular music, meant the trumpet was soon playing second fiddle to a guitar, just in time for the new genre of music that was about to change everything.

Rock and roll first exploded in Glasgow much the same way it did in the rest of the UK, via the use of Bill Haley and the Comets' 'Rock Around the Clock' in the soundtrack of the 1955 movie *Blackboard Jungle*. Originally the flip side of a failed single the previous year, the song now reached a wider audience via the movie and ushered rock and roll into the mainstream. When released as an A-side it topped the charts on both sides of the Atlantic and became the first single to sell over a million copies in the UK. Haley followed it up with a string of hits, including 'Shake, Rattle and Roll' and 'See You Later, Alligator', but the then thirty-year-old was hardly teen idol material and the younger, sexier Elvis Presley was waiting in the wings.

Closer to home, another seismic event was about to shake those digging the new beat, when a Glasgow-born, London-based jazz aficionado set out to demonstrate that music wasn't just for the moneyed. Lonnie Donegan took 'Rock Island Line', an American folk tune popularised by Leadbelly, and using cobbled-together instruments such as a washboard (younger readers, i.e., anyone under sixty, might need to look this one up), a tea-chest bass (ditto), and a cheap Spanish guitar, invented a folk-blues-rock hybrid called skiffle. For his efforts, he was rewarded with a top-ten single, with more to follow. Alex Harvey never really jumped on board the skiffle bandwagon (although there were some soon-to-be-famous young men in Liverpool who did), but the popular success of someone originally from Glasgow must have opened his eyes to a world of possibilities.

Harvey was more fascinated by the exotic new breed of American musicians, with 1956 seeing UK chart debuts for Presley, Little Richard, and Gene Vincent ('Heartbreak Hotel', 'Long Tall Sally' and 'Be-Bop-a-Lula' respectively). His interest must also have been piqued, however, by the arrival that same year of Britain's first rock and roll star, Tommy Steele, who hit number one with 'Singing the Blues' and thirteen with 'Rock With the Caveman'. Harvey would have been just one of many who thought that if a working-class boy from Bermondsey, London, could make it, then so too could he. His opportunity arrived in 1957 when Scottish tabloid *The Sunday Mail* announced a competition to find Scotland's answer to Tommy Steele. The winner was announced by David Gibson in the 28 April 1957 edition of the newspaper:

After seeing over 600 hopefuls in Aberdeen, Kirkcaldy, Inverness, Dundee, Glasgow, and Edinburgh, the judges in the *Sunday Mail*'s 'Search for Scotland's Tommy Steele' – theatrical impresario and bandleader Bill Patterson and myself – have reached our decision.

Scotland's Tommy Steele is 22-year-old Alex Harvey, of 462 Crown Street, Glasgow, a cooper at the docks.

Alex put up a wonderful performance at Glasgow's area final. He is a first-rate rock 'n' roll singer, but he is not limited to rock 'n' roll [here Gibson unwittingly outlines Harvey's career manifesto], and his vitality is unlimited.

Bill and I are glad a boy like Alex has won the prizes of £25, a film test and an audition with a recording company, because he is just an ordinary Glasgow lad. In fact, he's not as well-off as many.

Harvey's winning of this competition is usually used to illustrate how long it took for him to achieve mainstream success but is otherwise dismissed because Steele had the temerity to use his rock and roll success as a launchpad into a very long and successful career in film, television, and theatre. He has also enjoyed success as an artist, sculptor, and author. The cheek of the boy, eh?

However, it is worth putting Harvey's win in the context of 1957, when Steele was the hottest star in town, with four hit singles in the space of a year, including a number one, a top five album, and a biopic, *The Tommy Steele Story*, where, in a daring piece of casting, the title role was played by ... Tommy Steele. It was also rumoured that the Bermondsey Boy was earning more than Prime Minister Harold MacMillan.

In other words, beating off 600 other contenders to win this competition had the potential to be a Very Big Thing. Tomorrow surely belonged to the 'ordinary Glasgow lad' that had just been proclaimed Scotland's answer to the ludicrously successful Steele.

Alex Harvey and His Soul Band – Alex Harvey and His Soul Band

Personnel:
Alex Harvey: vocals and guitar
George Carmichael: saxophone
Bobby Thompson: bass
Other players unknown, but may include other members of Kingsize Taylor and the Dominoes, circa October 1963
Produced by Paul Murphy at Polydor Studio, Harvesterhuder Weg, Hamburg
Release Date: 1964
Label: Polydor Germany
Highest Chart Place: Did not chart
Running time: 41:12

Unfortunately, nothing appears to have come of the film test and record company audition that Alex won in the Tommy Steele competition – no biography even mentions them ever taking place – so 22-year-old Harvey, who would later claim to have had 36 jobs before becoming a musician, took on the role that would last to the end of his life, that of itinerant minstrel. He was married to Mary (*née* Martin), who worked, the *Sunday Mail* informed its readership, as a cinema usherette, and their son, Alex Jnr, would make his entry into the world in 1959. Bills had to be paid and food put on the table, so Alex hit the road.

One thing that had changed was how he billed himself. He had most recently been in the Kansas City Counts, which, if the occasion called for it, could be reduced to the Kansas City skiffle Group or, after donning gold lamé jackets, expanded to become the Kansas City Jazz Band. But having won the Tommy Steele contest, Harvey now wanted top billing and henceforth his name appeared front and centre on advertising (besides, too many smart-arses were scoring out the O in 'Counts'). There he was playing Whitecraig Hall in East Lothian on 25 May 1958, billed as Alex Harvey *and His Group*. Or there he was at the Rosewell Institute in Midlothian on 26 April 1959, performing as Alex Harvey *and His All-Star Band*. Or back at the same venue on 11 December, his musicians demoted simply to *& His Band*, and the main man still peddling the Scotland's Tommy Steele tag two and a half years on. Or, finally, there he is at Alloa Town Hall supporting Johnny Gentle and His Group on 20 May 1960, billed once again as 'Scotland's Own Tommy Steele' and now backed by *His Beat Band*. In other words, fame didn't come a-callin' in 1957, so Harvey spent the next several years playing not just here, there, and everywhere, but also hither and thither.

Despite the many band names it was largely the same players each time depending on availability, people like George McGowan on drums, Bill Patrick on sax, Jimmy Grimes on bass, and Robert Nimmo on rhythm guitar.

13

And speaking of line-ups, it would be churlish not to mention that Johnny Gentle's Group consisted of John Lennon, Paul McCartney, George Harrison, Stuart Sutcliffe, and Silver Beetles drummer for two months, Tommy Moore. And while I am in a 'pointing things out' frenzy, it is also worth noting that during these years of playing just about every village hall in Scotland, Harvey's band were regularly on a double bill with an outfit called the Sensational Saints (sometimes billed as the Sensational Saints Show Band). Perhaps Alex made note of his co-stars' hyperbolic adjective for future use.

Around this time, Alex became reacquainted with Bill Fehilly, an entrepreneur with an eye on the next money spinner. He and brother Dave spotted an opportunity during the construction of a power station at Dounreay in Caithness, then and now a remote area at the top of mainland Scotland. To attract workers to such an isolated site, the UK Atomic Energy Authority built attractive, modern, and affordable housing, and the Fehilly brothers were quick to realise that meant a lot of walls and rooms needed to be painted. With money made from their house-painting escapades, they opened cafes in Thurso and Wick that thrived with highland teenagers thanks to their well-stocked jukeboxes. Bill also dabbled in music promotion, attracting half-decent acts to the pop culture-starved north of Scotland, including Alex Harvey and whatever his band were called now. Harvey had initially known Fehilly back in Glasgow, where he would earn beer tokens by putting up posters for Fehilly's shows. Several sources state that Fehilly also became Harvey's manager around this time, but unfortunately, none say when this started or how long it lasted.

Harvey's career stalled at the local level, and in 1963, he followed The Beatles, The Searchers, and many others to Hamburg. His band were now called the Soul Band, which, according to Alan Clayson in his book *Hamburg: The Cradle of British Rock*, came not from the music genre associated with Stax and Motown but from an article Harvey had read in *Crescendo* magazine, which had used the term 'soul jazz' when describing the work of pianist Horace Silver. Harvey's band had been recruited by Ian Hines, a fellow Glaswegian whose band the Jets were the first British rock and rollers to play Germany's second biggest city (he was also the brother of future *Doctor Who* star Frazer Hines), who was now working as a scout for house-band fodder for The Star and Top Ten Clubs.

Despite famously gruelling schedules that could consist of up to six sets a day, Harvey's sense of showmanship was already in evidence, with the Soul Band decked out in silver lamé jackets with matching bow ties and white high-heeled boots. The *Last of the Teenage Idols* book quotes Harvey's memories of that time:

> Britain at that time was well drab. I mean, if you got a fish supper after 12 o'clock, that was really having a big night. If someone knew where to get a half bottle of wine on a Sunday – wow! You could go to this place,

Hamburg, where we lived 24 hours a day and could actually be in the same club, and play with Ray Charles, The Everly Brothers, Bo Diddley, The Ink Spots, Joey Dee & The Starliters, Jerry Lee Lewis, and Chuck Berry first hand. You'd look at that and think 'Now, last week we were in East Whitburn...'

Soon, Harvey and his Soul band were catching the attention of their fellow musicians, and it wasn't for their dress sense. Here are three of them, speaking in *Hamburg: The Cradle of British Rock*. **Tony Sheridan, who famously recorded some songs backed by the early Beatles, said that he:**

...wasn't impressed with the majority of groups from Liverpool. Though they were extremely attractive and charming, the music didn't come up to expectations. It was an affront to watch some of them when there were people like Alex Harvey, who came to the Top Ten with the first true rhythm and blues band I'd ever seen on stage. That knocked me out completely.

Ricky Barnes, a Hamburg mainstay and one of the teeming multitude whose band was composed of nameless All-Stars:

The Top Ten Club was a great place for young musicians. It made them three times, four times better than when they came in. Alex Harvey came across because there wasn't enough work for him in Scotland. He was way ahead of the competition, both as an experienced player and for his feel for the blues. None of the Liverpool groups had it – and I mean none of them – they were more like showbands. Alex built an atmosphere, it was a driving, swinging thing, and you could see the excitement on the faces of the crowd.

And finally, Mike Hart of Liverpool's Roadrunners:

The best R&B bands I ever saw were The Beatles, The Big Three, The Bobby Patrick Big Six, and The Alex Harvey Soul Band.

It wasn't just for his showmanship that Harvey stood out. In the rough and rowdy Reeperbahn, Alex gave truth to a Gorbals stereotype. Tony Sheridan recalled, 'Alex Harvey was a feared man. There was a table that ran from the stage down the length of the hall, and he once charged down it, kicking heads as he went.' Even Soul Band drummer George McGowan admitted things, and his frontman, could get out of hand. 'The band was kind of wild, so I held onto my cash in case I needed to get a flight home in a hurry. What was funny was that Alex was a conscientious objector' (true, he had registered as such in 1954) 'and yet he was always fighting all the time'.
  This doesn't sound at all like the 1970s model who would implore his audiences not to make, buy, or shoot bullets, and who was known to leave the stage from time to time to break up a fight in the crowd. And all that blood

and broken teeth is no way to look after one's shiny white booties. Presumably, the savage breast was sufficiently soothed when, on 3 October 1963, Harvey realised his long-held dream of cutting an album. He had already recorded some 45s for German jukeboxes, covers of 'Jailhouse Rock' and Little Richard's 'Hey-Hey-Hey-Hey!' under the title 'Going Back to Birmingham', but contractual reasons led to these singles being made under pseudonyms such as Bruce Wellington and his Robber Band. Those same contractual reasons meant that his debut long player *Alex Harvey and His Soul Band*, recorded for Polydor Germany, only featured two of the titular band, Harvey and saxophonist George Carmichael. The rest of the musicians were members of Liverpool outfit Kingsize Taylor and The Dominoes, who in their pre-Hamburg days counted Cilla Black among their members before solo success beckoned. Writing in *Record Collector* (2011), Alan Clayson states that the Soul Band album was completed in just twelve hours, 'from plug-in to final mix'.

Alex Harvey and His Soul Band is sometimes cited as 'Scotland's first rock album' (see, for example, *Mojo*, April 2000), but for that to work, one must conveniently overlook Lonnie Donegan and skiffle.

'Framed' (Jerry Leiber, Mike Stoller)

'Framed' is a 'talking blues' song, first recorded as a 1954 B-side by American doo-wop group, The Robins, and despite appearing on Ritchie Valens' debut album four years later, it was still an obscurity when Harvey added it to his setlist.

This version opens with the sound of applause, which, according to Tim Barr in the book that accompanies the *Last of the Teenage Idols* box set, was supplied by the musicians in the studio to create the illusion of a concert recording. Although as brass-driven as the original, Harvey, approximating an American accent and replacing the Henry of the original lyric with his own name, follows the slower arrangement of the Valens version and adopts some of Valens' hesitant phraseology. Alex was obviously pleased with the results, as the song would reappear as the title track of the Sensational Alex Harvey Band's debut album.

'I Ain't Worrying Baby' (Harvey)

The first Harvey original committed to record is the most then-contemporary track on the album, one aligned to the British beat boom of the 1960s that could equally have been raising temperatures at lunch-time concerts in Liverpool's Cavern as it was at the Kaiserkeller or Top Ten Club in Hamburg. The only concession to the Soul Band's usual sound on this up-tempo Beatle-esque number is the faintly flatulent sax accompaniment.

'Backwater Blues' (Lonnie Johnson)

Although credited to Lonnie Johnson (after whom Harvey's fellow Glaswegian Lonnie Donegan named himself), this song was written in 1927 by Bessie

Smith. Johnson recorded it on his 1960 album *Blues & Ballads* where the correct authorship was given. Similar discrepancies occur with many of the song credits here, but for the sake of consistency, I have retained the names credited on the album sleeve and label.

Although the actual Soul Band doesn't play on the record, their job as a live act was to keep the punters dancing and, by extension, drinking, so they and their studio doppelgängers ditch the dirge of Smith's piano original and Lonnie's guitar lament in favour of something altogether jauntier, making this reading of 'Backwater Blues' the happiest song about a natural disaster that caused huge loss of life, homes and livelihoods (the Christmas Day flooding of Nashville, Tennessee in 1926).

'Let the Good Times Roll' (Leonard Lee)
Despite what the credit says, this is not the sweet 1956 single by Shirly and Lee (and if it were, the songwriting credit should go to both performers) but is instead the twelve-bar blues written by Sam Theard and Fleecie Moore and first recorded by Louis Jordan in 1946.

'This was a beautiful old song until we got our hands on it', quips Harvey at the beginning of the faux Soul Band's version, but despite some Stax-style raucousness, they remain true to the pace and primitivism of the original.

'Going Home' (Harvey)
'Going Home' is a slice of horn-heavy, finger-snappin', zippy four beats to the bar R&B. There is nothing particularly original about it, but that's no surprise as it would have been written to complement the covers that comprised the bulk of Harvey's set.

'Got My Mojo Working' (McKinley Morganfield)
Ya'll know the drill by now: Despite what it says above, McKinley Morganfield, AKA Muddy Waters, did not write this song, that honour belonging to Preston 'Red' Foster. The man called Muddy did record the best-known version in 1957, however, a year after its composition, throwing in an extra line or two in the process.

Superficial changes based on the composition of the band aside, Harvey and company don't detour any from the Muddy Waters version or, indeed, Ann Cole's '56 original.

'Teensville USA' (Wayne Cogswell)
The original version of this was recorded by Chet Atkins on his 1960 platter of the same name, and in places veers suspiciously close to 'When the Saints Go Marching In'. Harvey's Soul Band rendition adds 'USA' to the title, drops the vocals, and replaces the guitar with saxophone, leaving the end result sounding nothing like that old spiritual or, surprisingly, Chet Atkins'

'Teensville'. My best guess is they needed another number to fill the vinyl, played the Atkins' original, tried it once, and declared it close enough, even though it really isn't.

'New Orleans' (Traditional)

'New Orleans' is not the traditional song the credit states, but was written by Frank Guida and Joseph Royster, and originally recorded by Gary U. S. Bonds a mere four years before *Alex Harvey and His Soul Band* was released. A perennial crowd pleaser with its call and response 'Hey-hey-ey-ey-yeah', it has been recorded many times by artists as diverse as the Ventures, Neil Diamond, Gillan, Dr John, Joan Jett and the Blackhearts, and, coming off the back of the successful *Tutti Frutti* television series, Robbie Coltrane. The Harvey Band were early entrants in the field, their take sticking close to the U. S. Bonds original, although Harvey's vocals should have been higher in the mix.

'Bo Diddley is a Gunslinger' (Bo Diddley)

The 'Bo Diddley Beat' of the original is played down, but this is an otherwise faithful if poorly mixed reading of the title track of the second of Bo Diddley's 1960 album releases.

'When I Grow Too Old to Rock' (Sigmund Romberg, Oscar Hammerstein II)

This is a retitled take of 'When I Grow Too Old to Dream', a song that originally appeared in the 1935 Ramon Novarro movie *The Night is Young*, and demonstrates Harvey's eclecticism when it came to cover songs was there from day one. Harvey dispenses with the original's ballad arrangement, giving this an up-tempo rockabilly beat.

'Evil Hearted Man' (Josh White)

Harvey takes Josh White's original, drops the leisurely-paced blues guitar in favour of piano and saxophone, and cranks up the pace to make the cats go, man, go. The trouble is, he has been doing that with just about every song on this album, and by the time the listener gets to this, each track begins bleeding into the next.

'I Just Wanna Make Love to You' (Willie Dixon)

Having first been committed to vinyl by the man called Muddy in 1954, this Willie Dixon classic was already well on its way to becoming a standard by the time the Soul Band got their hands on it a mere ten years later. Their cover, which was released as the Soul Band's debut single, is a surprisingly laid-back lounge reading lacking the raucousness of earlier versions, such as the one Etta James delivers on her *At Last!* long player, and finally, allows *this* album a long overdue change of pace.

'The Blind Man' (Traditional)

This version of the traditional spiritual, featuring Harvey solo on voice and guitar, acts as a perfect counterbalance to all the sweaty r 'n' r 'n' r 'n' b that preceded it, and adds some colour to an album that was in danger of being dangerously black and white. Harvey would often perform this solo as an encore at Soul Band gigs.

Related Songs
'Reeling and Rocking' (Chuck Berry)

This bonus track was slapped on the 1980s reissue of *Alex Harvey and His Soul Band* and follows the template of much of the original album, that is, faithful run-throughs of other artists' songs, with added sax.

'Going Back to Birmingham' (Richard Penniman)

This faithful if retitled version of Little Richard's 'Hey-Hey-Hey-Hey', the B-side of 'Good Golly Miss Molly' was recorded by The Sabres and appeared on the album *Everything's Allright* (sic) *With Isabella Bond*. It was also a fixture on early '60s Hamburg jukeboxes. The Sabres was a pseudonym for Harvey and his band.

'Jailhouse Rock' (Jerry Leiber, Mike Stoller)

Another straight reading cover of an early rock classic, another track from both *Everything's Allright With Isabella Bond* and local jukeboxes, and another phony name for the Soul Band, this time James Dale and the Top Ten Allstars.

The Blues – Alex Harvey

Personnel:
Alex Harvey: vocals and guitar
Leslie Harvey: guitar
Produced by Paul Murphy at Studio Rahlstedt, Hamburg, 8-10 May 1964
Release Date: 1965
Label: Polydor
Highest Chart Place: Did not chart
Running time: 35.42

When a given entry is backed up by citations and links to sources, Wikipedia is a wonderful resource. When this is not the case, it can be more problematic. Case in point, this entry for the second Alex Harvey album *The Blues*:

> Originally *The Blues* would have been the third album, but Polydor did not release the second one. Rumour has it that Alex was not happy about this and paid them back with a commercial disaster by making this acoustic album. The sleeve notes on the back tell that it was the idea of Paul Murphy (producer of the Soul Band's debut) to make the album, but it was Alex who insisted, and Polydor had to agree.

The problem with this is that *The Blues* was recorded before the unreleased 'second' album was even completed. By this time, the Soul Band were playing the London circuit, but some cancelled dates led to unexpected free time, so Alex and young brother Les – who had been playing in his big brother's old band the Kinning Park Ramblers – set off for Hamburg, at the request of Paul Murphy, who thought an acoustic blues album might highlight Harvey's talent better than another full band effort. The dates of the recording sessions, which featured the Harvey brothers as the album's sole musicians, were 8-10 May 1964. Recording on the second Soul Band album began much earlier, on 2 September 1963, but was not completed until 14 August 1964, by which time *The Blues* was in the can and Harvey's Hamburg days were behind him.

Unfortunately, not everyone – or, indeed, *anyone* – shared Murphy's enthusiasm for Harvey's ability, and it didn't help that the album wasn't released until November 1965, a full year and a half after it was recorded and a month before some of his old Hamburg colleagues released *Rubber Soul*. By the time *The Blues* made it to record shelves it was already hopelessly outdated and sank without a trace.

'Trouble in Mind' (Richard M. Jones)
'Trouble in Mind' is a vaudeville blues song first recorded by Thelma La Vizzo in 1924, with the song's composer Richard Jones on piano. It has been covered umpteen times in the succeeding century, by artists as diverse as Bob Wills and His Texas Playboys, Nina Simone, Sam Cooke, the Everly

Brothers, Val Doonican, and any number of ensembles ending in the words 'Jug Band'. The Harvey Brothers' version is just one more take, with nothing to distinguish it from the rest.

'Honey Bee' (Muddy Waters)
There's that man Muddy again, slapping some new words on Bumble Bee Slim's 'Sail On, Little Girl, Sail On', and calling it his own. And here's the Harv, covering yet another Muddy Waters song, possibly even the first to remake this particular number, but it still sounds like something we've all heard before.

'I Learned About Women' (Rudyard Kipling, Jimmy Grimes)
This is a musical adaptation of Rudyard Kipling's 1922 poem 'The Ladies' by Harvey's old Soul Bandmate Jimmy Grimes and is more traditional Scottish folk than blues. As we shall see, Harvey apparently recognised that an LP's worth of acoustic blues might lack enough variety to keep the listener engaged, so was willing to dabble in other genres despite the album's title.

Harvey would return to the Grimes tune in 1977 and set his own lyrics to it for the song 'No Complaints Department'.

'Danger Zone' (Percy Mayfield)
This was composed in 1961 by Percy Mayfield when he was essentially working as a private songwriter for Ray Charles, and appeared on the flip side of Charles' US number one 'Hit the Road Jack', also penned by Mayfield. Harvey takes Charles' sparse jazzy ballad and gives it an equally sparse, bluesy arrangement.

Les Harvey would revisit this song on the second Stone the Crows album *Ode to John Law* (1970).

'The Riddle Song' (Traditional; arranged by Harvey)
Some of Harvey's choices for this album have long histories, but none more so than this, which began life in fifteenth-century England and is also known by the alternative title 'I Gave My Love A Cherry'. The opening lyric, 'I gave my love a cherry without a stone' has often and unsurprisingly been taken as a reference to the hymen, but the New Shorter Oxford English Dictionary states the slang use of cherry in that sense is not attested until the early twentieth century. Additionally, to proscribe that meaning to the opening line is to conveniently overlook the narrator's other gifts, such as a chicken without a bone and a story with no end. It is called 'The Riddle Song' for a reason.

An eclectic host of worthies have recorded 'The Riddle Song', including Burl Ives, Pete Seeger, Sam Cooke, Joan Baez, Val Doonican (again!), and fellow '70s Saturday night favourite Nana Mouskouri, but if the title is unfamiliar, then the melody almost certainly will be. Both Johnny Mathis and Donny Osmond topped the UK charts with it after Jerry Livingston and Paul Webster wrote new lyrics and called it 'The Twelfth of Never'.

Harvey plays the song straight and produces an airy, acoustic pop ballad with a warm vocal. Manager David Firmstone and Polydor were reputedly trying to coax Alex into crooner territory around this time, and 'The Riddle Song' may be seen as evidence of that ploy; whether this was the case or not, it is the album's standout track.

'Waltzing Matilda' (Banjo Paterson, Marie Cowan)
Harvey maintains his distance from the blues with this countrified reading of Australia's unofficial national anthem, but unfortunately, it lacks the melancholy inherent in the better versions of the song and is one of the weakest tracks.

'T.B. Blues' (Jimmie Rodgers)
Jimmie Rodgers composed this ode to his illness a mere two years before it claimed him in 1933 at the age of 35, but still managed to lend it a lightness with its country-blues arrangement and partial yodelling. Harvey throws all that out, resulting in a plodding, doom-laden dirge that is almost a blues caricature. It ties with 'Waltzing Matilda' as the album's nadir.

'The Big Rock Candy Mountain' (Traditional; arranged by Harvey)
Having eschewed the country aspects in the previous track, Harvey embraces it in his reading of this American folk song, which is often described as traditional but may have been written by Harry McClintock in the late nineteenth century; he certainly recorded the first version in 1928.

The lyrics concern a hobo searching for a place where 'handouts grow on bushes', there are 'cigarette trees' and 'little streams of alcohol', and bulldogs have rubber teeth; in other words, an American West equivalent of Cockaigne, the mythical mediaeval land of plenty. There are more sanitised versions for children, with soda pop lakes replacing whiskey ones for example, and that's what Harvey opts for here, with both his vocal delivery and simple arrangement also suggesting he was singing this for kids. As such, it is an odd inclusion on this album and makes it the third miss in a row.

'The Michigan Massacre' (Woody Guthrie)
Woody Guthrie's song '1913 Massacre' gets a title change, a slightly brisker arrangement, and a couple of verses conflated into one, but Harvey otherwise adheres to the original. It is a solid if non-stellar version, but something of a relief after the three preceding tracks.

'No Peace' (A. Harvey, Leslie Harvey)
The first of two originals by the Harvey brothers, this has an authentic vintage ring to it, but it also sounds like something that was written by people whose record collection consisted of just one Muddy Waters album.

'Nobody Knows You When You're Down and Out' (Jimmie Cox)

With its hints of vaudeville and ragtime, one can hear the Twenties roaring from the grooves of the 1923 Jimmie Cox original. The same can be said of Bessie Smith's arguable definitive version recorded six years later and mere months before the Wall Street Crash brought down the curtains on the decade-long party. By the time Harvey gets to it, 'Nobody Knows You' has become an oft-recorded blues standard, many of which ditch the piano in favour of the guitar, as Alex does here. As such, the musical DNA of the original is diluted, and it becomes just another blues song.

'St. James Infirmary' (Joe Primrose)

Joe Primrose was a pseudonym for Irving Mills, but did he really write 'St. James Infirmary' or was it a chap called Don Redman? For that matter, what is the actual title of this song? Is it simply 'St. James Infirmary', or is it 'St. James Infirmary Blues', or 'Gambler's Blues', or 'Those Gambler's Blues'? And did it really start life as an English folksong called 'The Unfortunate Rake'?

The point is, the convoluted history of the song is considerably more fascinating that the song itself. Harvey's rendition is okay, but it does nothing to stand out from the multitude of versions that preceded it.

'Strange Fruit' (Lewis Allan)

Like 'St. James Infirmary', 'Strange Fruit' has an interesting back story. It was originally a poem by DeWitt Clinton English high school teacher Abel Meeropel, who published it under the pseudonym Lewis Allan. Meeropel, a white Jewish New Yorker far removed from the American South, was moved to write the poem after seeing – and being 'haunted' by – Lawrence Beitler's horrific 1930 photo of the lynching of Thomas Shipp and Abram Smith in Marion, Indiana. The poem depicts a Southern pastoral where the bodies of lynched black men, the titular 'fruit' of the title, hang amidst the 'Scent of magnolia, sweet and fresh'. He later set the poem to music, performing it in clubs with his wife and singer Laura Duncan, and its growing reputation brought it to the attention of Billie Holiday.

Unlike 'St. James Infirmary', Harvey adapts the song rather than doing a straight cover version, upping the pace a few notches from the funeral dirge of Holiday's original and singing it in a dramatic rather than world-weary tone. Did Alex choose to record this because, like 'The Michigan Massacre' and 'The Ballad of John F. Kennedy', it allowed him to rail against injustice and abusive authoritarianism, or does its 1964 recording indicate a cognisance with the quickening pulse of the American Civil Rights movement? With all the players long gone, we will never know.

Incidentally, Abel Meeropel and his wife Anne later scored further good guy points by adopting the children of Julius and Ethel Rosenberg after their parents were executed for espionage in 1953. The Meeropels were unrelated to the Rosenbergs, but offered to adopt Michael and Robert Rosenberg when it became clear their many relatives refused to.

'Kisses Sweeter Than Wine' (Joel Newman, Paul Campbell)

Paul Campbell was a pseudonym used by the original members of American folk group the Weavers (Ronnie Gilbert, Lee Hays, Fred Hellerman, and Pete Seeger) and Joel Newman was a pseudonym of the already pseudonymous Leadbelly. Other sources state that both names were pseudonyms of the Weavers' publisher, Howie Richmond. Either way, the song started life as Irish folk tune 'Drimindown', about a farmer and his cow, a theme Leadbelly kept when he gave the tune new lyrics and called it 'If It Wasn't For Dicky'. Along came the Weavers, who gave both farmer and cow their marching orders, and transformed the herding ditty into the love song 'Kisses Sweeter Than Wine'. Harvey turns in a version that doesn't stray far from the Weavers original, even retaining its sweetness.

'Good God Almighty' (A. Harvey, L. Harvey)

See 'No Peace' above.

Abandoned Second Alex Harvey and His Soul Band Album – Alex Harvey and His Soul Band

Personnel:
Alex Harvey: vocals and guitar
Robert Nimmo: guitar
Jimmie Grimes: bass
George McGowan: drums
George Carmichael: saxophone
Bill Patrick: saxophone
Produced by Paul Murphy in Hamburg and Lansdowne Studios, London
Release Date: Unreleased until 1999
Label: Polydor (1964)/Bear Family Records (1999)
Highest Chart Place: Did not chart
Running time: 46.17

Hamburg, or more specifically the St. Pauli area of the city in which all the now-famous clubs clustered, may have meant long shifts, low wages, and shitty accommodation, but it offered British musicians a sleazy neon bohemia of sex and drugs and rock and roll unimaginable in their dreary old homeland. Clubs that catered for live rock and roll were still a rarity back in Blighty, so it also offered an opportunity for bands to hone both their musicianship and their stagecraft before a live audience. What it didn't necessarily offer, however, was career advancement. For every Beatles, there was a Downliners Sect, a Johnnie Law and the MI5, a Blue Diamonds, a Kingsize Taylor and the Dominoes, or indeed, an Alex Harvey and His Soul Band, and many more besides.

With this in mind, the Soul Band packed their bags and headed to the place that could help take them to the next level, London, making their debut in the capital at the newly rechristened 100 Club on 6 February 1964 (it had previously been called the Feldman Swing Club). In July, they performed at a benefit night at the Marquee honouring Mark Leeman of the Mark Leeman Five, who had been killed in a car crash the previous month. The Soul Band came on after resident band Jimmy James and the Vagabonds, whereupon, according to *Melody Maker*'s Nick Jones, the audience were treated to 'slightly harsher soul sounds' than those provided by Mr James and company. Unit Four+Two, Manfred Mann and the Animals populated the upper echelons of the bill.

Other gigs found the band, now invariably billed as The Alex Harvey Soul Band, helping the Rolling Stones celebrate the success of their first Top Ten single, 'Not Fade Away', at Windsor Ex-Servicemen's Club, and opening in January 1965 for Rod Stewart and The Soul Agents at the Marquee. This gig got them noticed and bagged them a residency at the famed club supporting Rod's old boss, Long John Baldry, complete with his Hoochie Coochie Men, an engagement that led to Harvey meeting his second wife Trudy.

Trudy Harvey recalled the occasion for the *Glasgow Herald*'s Russell Leadbetter in 2016:

'I must have been about 17 or 18. I went to see Long John Baldry. The Soul Band were the support group. I went with someone who knew Alex vaguely, and she introduced me to him. But prior to that, when I saw the performance, I thought he was an amazing performer. He put me in mind of a kind of highwayman. He was so charismatic.

'The band were very Glaswegian. It was all 'get that fuckin' gear on the fuckin' stand, for fuck's sake', that kind of language. I come from Leigh-on-Sea in Essex, and it sounds so crazy now, but I had hardly heard that word before. But I remember watching them and thinking, 'This is interesting'. The Soul Band were brilliant: I loved that kind of music'.

Late 1964 or early 1965 should have seen the release of the second Soul Band album – and the first to feature the actual Soul Band. Unlike the done-in-twelve-hours approach to the first album, this had been a work in progress since autumn 1963 and was finally concluded in August 1964. For reasons unknown, Polydor chose not to release it and buried it in their vault, and it only saw the light of day three and a half decades later courtesy of Bear Family Records.

'Shout' (Ronald Isley, Rudolph Isley, O'Kelly Isley Jr.)
Alex Harvey and the Soul Band first heard the Isley Brothers' original on a jukebox in a café in the rock and roll heartland of, um, Wick, in the far north of Scotland, and, after upping the song's already frantic urgency, it soon became a showstopping staple of their live show. When they recorded it they added equally feverish but sweet teen siren backing vocals, a winning combination that the band strangely never used again. 'Shout' was presumably intended as a single but ended up lost in the same vault as its parent album.

But someone from Harvey's hometown had taken note of his version. In the 2002 television programme, *An Audience With Lulu*, the former Marie McDonald McLaughlan Lawrie recalled: 'I went to see him at a little club called The Scene. Alex got up on stage, and he was like the Beatles of Scotland. It was a cult thing. He wore all black leather and was very hairy and skinny from working in Germany for months. He went on stage and did 'Shout'. I stood there with my mouth open, I just couldn't believe it'. Talking to *Reader's Digest* in 2019, Lulu confirmed she was 'blown away' by the raw energy he imbued the song with. 'I had to put the song in my act'. She was more succinct with Chris Welch of *Melody Maker* in 1973: 'When I was 13 I pinched 'Shout' from Alex Harvey'.

The Harvey version served as the template for Lulu and the Luvvers' debut single, which reached number seven in 1964. Fair enough; the 'little lady with the BIG voice' was probably easier to pitch than the 'scary mutha with the pitch-black crazy eyes'.

It may all sound a bit dog-eat-dog, but in her defence, Lulu has remained a staunch supporter of Harvey. Here she is talking to *Bèatscene* in August 1964, just after both singers had migrated to London: 'I'm glad Alex Harvey is going down so well here too. Along with Ray Charles, he's my favourite singer, and on the London scene, I'm not the only one who thinks he's great'. A decade later, she was telling *Melody Maker,* 'He was my idol, you know. He was the greatest rock and roll singer I heard in my life'. And finally, on *An Audience With Lulu*: 'It kills me that he never did have the breaks, but when he was hot, he was hot'.

Fun fact: Lulu was born in Lennox Castle Hospital, Lennoxtown, as was Ted McKenna of the Sensational Alex Harvey Band. My mate Jim O'Donnell was also born there, but that is a totally indulgent shout-out that will probably rightly get edited out as he isn't part of this story.

'Sticks and Stones' (Traditional)
This 'traditional' song was actually written by Henry Glover and Titus Turner, the latter of which also recorded it. It was a big hit for Ray Charles in 1960 and it is his version the Soul Band follow here.

'Take Out Some Insurance On Me Baby' (Waldense J. Hall, Charles Singleton)
First recorded by electric bluesman Jimmy Reed in 1959, 'Take Out Some Insurance' arguably gained its greatest prominence when recorded by the young Beatles in 1961 in their capacity as Tony Sheridan's backing band in Hamburg. Although unreleased at the time, it and everything else they recorded with Sheridan was made available in the wake of the Beatles' success.

The lyrics were rewritten somewhere between the Reed original and the 1961 Sheridan remake (by whom is unknown), and Harvey plumps for the new version, no doubt because Sheridan was still knocking it out in Hamburg when Harvey was there, even if his backing band had moved on. Alex delivers a convincing Mississippi delta vocal, which begs the question: why go for this when you could just as easily purchase a version by someone from Mississippi?

'Long Long Gone' (Alex Harvey)
In one respect, Harvey and the Soul Band had been doing precisely what the Beatles, the Rolling Stones, and the Kinks had been doing. Record a Bo Diddley song? Tick. Jimmy Reed? Tick. Chuck Berry, and so on. Where Harvey failed to emulate his contemporaries was not only in neglecting to make the switch fully to original material, but also in failing to write compositions strong enough to chime with the now. There is no 'Do You Want to Know a Secret' or 'There's a Place', 'no 'You Really Got Me' or 'Stob Your Sobbing'. The Stones were admittedly a bit late out of the trap when it came to original

27

material, but once they got their mojo working, they turned into a two-man classic song factory. Going by 'Long Long Gone', Harvey seemed content to produce material that fitted in with his cover versions rather than standing out from them.

'Penicillin Blues' (Carr, O'Connor, Leach)

Regardless of the names given in the credits, 'Penicillin Blues' was co-written by the longstanding songwriting team of Brownie McGhee and Sonny Terry. The Soul Band give it a sparse but slinky late-night groove and Alex sings in his best Transatlantic, but this sophisticated sheen can't disguise the 'ooh-err, missus' *Carry On* crudity of the lyrics. Sample: 'Please stop wriggling, baby/'Cos you're going to break my needle off'.

'Shakin' All Over' (Johnny Kidd)

Well, here is a nice surprise. After being overly faithful when covering other people's songs thus far, Harvey goes in the complete opposite direction to produce a version of Johnny Kidd and The Pirates' 1960 smash that is not only all but unrecognisable but is utterly bonkers into the bargain. In doing so, he inadvertently invents the technique, popular in the late 1970s, of 'punking up' a song, that is, taking a well-known number and squeezing it into as short as time as possible. The singer would revisit 'Shakin' All Over' on 1979's *The Mafia Stole My Guitar*, giving it a different punked-up arrangement, but this reading is the better of the two.

    Fun fact: Respected session guitarist Joe Moretti achieved the distinctive guitar sound on 'Shakin' All Over' by sliding a cigarette lighter up and down the fretboard. He also played on two other UK number-one singles, Tom Jones' 'It's Not Unusual', and Chris Farlowe's 'Out of Time'. What, you might well be asking, has this to do with the price of mince? Just this: Joe Moretti came second in the *Daily Record*'s search for the Scottish Tommy Steele.

'Outskirts of Town' (William Weldon)

Casey Bill Weldon's minimalistic 1936 Piedmont original gets a sloppy band arrangement so loose it could go undercover in a late-night jazz joint.

'Tutti Frutti' (Richard Penniman, Dorothy La Bostrie, Joe Lubin)

Harvey loses the wop-bop-a-loo-bop-a-wop-bom-bom of Little Richard's 1955 hit and plays a version that owes as much to country swing as rock and roll.

'My Kind of Lovin'' (Alex Harvey)

This is a catchy post-Beat number that fits well into the British pop zeitgeist of 1965 when groups such as Manfred Mann, The Hollies, Herman's Hermits, and Unit 4+2 emerged to join The Beatles, the Stones, and the Kinks. 'My Kind of Lovin'' might not be the trawler, but unlike 'Long Long Gone' it is at least one of the seagulls closest to it, although Harvey is still arranging his material for a dated '50s American rock and roll band line-up complete with honking saxes, rather than a lither twin guitar, bass, and drum approach. The drumming on this track, presumably by Soul Band regular George McGowan, is fantastic.

Incredibly, the powers that be at Polydor Records tucked 'My Kind of Lovin" away on the flipside of the 'Ain't That Just Too Bad' single (see below) when it really should have been the lead track.

'Parchman Farm' (Mose Allison, Randy Cierley)
Ever wondered what it would sound like if Joe Meek teamed up with the Pirates to sing the blues? Wonder no more.

'Ten A Penny' (Alex Harvey, Peters)
This isn't of the same standard as 'My Kind of Lovin", but give it a big brassy, orchestrated arrangement and it could have been a perfect vehicle for Lulu, Cilla Black, or even Shirley Bassey.

'Canoe Song' (Mischa Spoliansky, Arthur Wimperis)
Here is another perfect example of Harvey's eclecticism when it came to song choices. 'Canoe Song' is an obscurity originally sung by American bass-baritone Paul Robeson in the 1935 British movie *Sanders of the River*, in which Robeson co-starred. Whereas Robeson sang with gravitas, Harvey gives the song a genteel folky makeover in the style of then-current hitmakers The Seekers or Peter, Paul and Mary, and it works just fine.

'You Ain't No Good to Me' (Alex Harvey)
This '50s throwback must count as one of the least compositions in the Harvey canon. It is the sort of song one forgets while it is still playing.

'You've Put a Spell On Me' (Alex Harvey)
Despite the title change, the lyric change, and the change in tempo, this still sounds suspiciously like 'I Put a Spell on You' by Screamin' Jay Hawkins, so I am not sure Harvey warrants the songwriting credit. I love the vocal intro, but Hawkins did that too; same but different. So, it is too derivative if it is an original, but if a cover, then kudos to the Harv for doing something different with it, and then points off for not giving Hawkins due credit.

'Hoochie Coochie Man' (Willie Dixon)
Willie wrote it, Muddy released it first, Long John Baldry named his band after it, and a million other white blues boys recorded it. Here's the Harvey take, which is neither the best nor the worst, but does demonstrate that Alex had a set of pipes well suited to the genre.

Related songs

'Elevator Rock' (Tommy Steele)

Scotland's Tommy Steele covers the actual Tommy Steele, kind of. Recorded during the first Soul Band album sessions, Harvey takes the flipside of Tommy's 1956 flop 'Doomsday Rock' and adds just a touch more zip and, for reasons unknown, an entirely different set of lyrics.

'You Are My Sunshine' (Jimmie Davis, Charles Mitchell)

Although now credited to publishers Davis and Mitchell, who copyrighted the song in 1940, the composer of 'You Are My Sunshine' remains unknown. The first known recording was by the Pine Ridge Boys in 1939, after which it quickly became a country music staple, but has since been recorded by a dizzying array of artists in a variety of styles. Harvey throws out all the country trappings, boosts the tempo and the phrasing, and gives the song a rocking Fifties soundtrack, meaning that while entertaining, it already sounded hopelessly out of date by the time he recorded it in 1964.

'Ain't That Just Too Bad'

The writer of this song goes uncredited on both the 1999 Bear Family CD release of the second Soul Band album and its inclusion in the *Last of the Teenage Idols* box set, but a quick look on discogs.com reveals the name Tennant, possibly Archie Tennant, who had previously written for Chet Atkins.

The Harvey version blends British beat group with Memphis R&B resulting in the proverbial neither fish nor fowl, but Polydor clearly thought a song that tapped into two successful genres was a sure-fire winner and released it as a single in July 1965. It wasn't, and it proved to be Alex's Polydor swan song.

'The Little Boy that Santa Claus Forgot' (Michael Carr, Tommie Connor, James Leach)

Harvey's mid-Sixties manager David Firmstone briefly entertained the notion that Alex could become an all-round entertainer or a crooner in the Englebert Humperdinck mould, and this recording from August 1964 sounds like a concerted effort to move in that direction. It is all chimes, plucked guitar, and Hollywood-styled choir, and those elements combined with Harvey's straight delivery means that it wouldn't look shifty in a police line-up comprising versions of this song by Billy Cotton and His Band, Nat 'King' Cole, Vera Lynn, and Anita Harris.

'Agent 00 Soul' (Charles Hatcher, Bill Sharpley)

The Edwin Starr original was going great guns in the US but doing nothing in Britain, so Alex, now signed to Fontana, fancied his chances with it. Despite a strong song, an exuberant performance by Harvey, Spencer Davis Group member Steve Winwood on the ivories, and the obvious tie-in with the then-James Bond fad, it joined the Starr version in British oblivion.

'Go Away Baby' (Harvey)

The British Blues Boom, exemplified by bands such as Blues Incorporated and John Mayall's Bluesbreakers, was in full swing by the time this was recorded, and Harvey clearly had taken note, updating his blues sound to swing with it.

Roman Wall Blues – Alex Harvey

Personnel:
Alex Harvey: vocals and guitar
Leslie Harvey: guitar
Mickey Keene: guitar
Bud Parkes: trumpet
Derek Watkins: trumpet
Derek Wadsworth: trombone, brass arrangements
Frank Ricotti: alto saxophone, percussion, brass arrangements
Ashton Tootell: baritone saxophone, flute
Laurie Baker: bass guitar, electronic effects
Maurice Cockerill: keyboards
Peter Woolf: drums
Produced at Philips (Phonogram) Studio, London, by Brian Shepherd and Alex Harvey
Release Date: October 1969
Label: Fontana
Highest Chart Place: Did not chart
Running time: 39:41

By 1965 it was clear that success and the Soul Band were a twain fated never to meet, and a disheartened Alex Harvey headed back to Glasgow. By the following year, he had formed The Alex Harvey Band, which became the house band on Friday and Saturday nights at the Dennistoun Palais. The line-up featured Alex and brother Les on guitars and Soul Band alumnus Bill Patrick on saxophone, and was rounded off by Dougie Paul (bass) and Miff Paterson (drums). An unusual feature of the band was that it had three lead vocalists. Joining Alex front and centre were George Gallacher, lead singer of the Poets, another Glasgow band for whom opportunity didn't knock, and old Hamburg pal Isobel (formerly Isabella) Bond.

It was hardly the bright lights of London, or even the sleaze pits of Hamburg, but it was steady money. However, Glasgow's dancin' days were nearly done, and even the venerable Palais, the city's biggest dancehall, was marked for closure and conversion to a roller-skating rink.

In 1967, Alex permanently relocated to London, a move that ended his marriage to Mary Harvey, who didn't share her husband's enthusiasm for the 'Big Smoke' and preferred to stay in Glasgow. His first musical venture was an outfit called Giant Moth, a name presumably inspired by the monster in the 1961 Japanese movie *Mothra*. The line-up consisted of two former members of a Kilmarnock band called the Anteeks, Jim Condron (bass) and George Butler (drums), along with Mox Gowland (flute, harmonica) and Alex (guitar, vocals). The music was folksy psychedelia with an on-trend eastern tinge, and they cut one excellent single for Decca and one so-so one before going their separate ways.

Alex was now living with his future second wife Trudy in a house on Redington Road, Hampstead – where fellow struggler David Bowie was a regular visitor – and was making his living as a jobbing musician, playing Leicester Square nightclubs such as the Eden Roc Club. It was through playing these venues that he got to know Derek Wadsworth. Wadsworth, too, was earning his crust on the cabaret and club circuit but had worked previously as Dusty Springfield's musical director and, in 1968, was offered the same role for the London production of *Hair*, the counterculture's first piece of musical theatre. Thanks to Wadsworth, Harvey became one of the London production's original 'tribe', which opened on 27 September 1968, alongside upcoming talent such as Elaine Page, Paul Nicholas, Richard O'Brien, Tim Curry, Sonja Kristina, Marsha Hunt, Floella Benjamin, and Oliver Tobias. For a short period of time, Harvey's 'understudy' was Mike Oldfield, but the young guitarist claims he deliberately got himself fired because he was bored after ten performances, which is a bit rich coming from the man that unleashed *Incantations* upon the world.

Harvey was a vocalist and guitarist in the 'Hairband', which unlike a traditional orchestra was not hidden away in the pit but was on stage along with the actors. He would also play a prominent role in the 'be-in' finale, where the tribe were joined onstage by members of the audience in a run-through of popular songs of the day. Being part of *Hair* offered a steady income but with Trudy now pregnant Harvey boosted his earnings by maintaining his nightclub work, hot-footing it from Shaftsbury Theatre to Soho at the end of the show. Being in a successful West End production offered Alex more than just financial rewards, as it also put him in touch with a pool of musicians he would return to time and again over the rest of his career. It also broadened his knowledge; studying the American creative team behind *Hair* gave Harvey greater insight into musical arrangement, presentation, theatricality, bridging the gap between stage and audience, discipline and professionalism.

During his *Hair* period, Alex also found himself in the recording studio on a regular basis. He appeared on both the original London cast's recording of *Hair* (1968) and its cash-in offspring *Hair Rave-Up* the following year. He also cropped up as a member of Ray Russell's Rock Workshop collective on their eponymous album in 1970, and these two last-named will be discussed later. In amongst all this activity, he also recorded his first solo album in five years, *Roman Wall Blues*, working with musicians from the Hairband and brother Leslie.

'Midnight Moses' (Harvey)
Roman Wall Blues opens with a song that will be instantly familiar to all fans of the Sensational Alex Harvey Band, and the version presented here is no less sensational than the one that would crop up on *Framed*. This take has a lovely percussive introduction by drummer Pete Woolf, before the not-inconsiderable brass section come in with that big, pumping riff that is surely

one of rock's best. The singer has not yet adopted the syllable-mangling Glaswegian accent that will characterise his Seventies work, nor does he retain the all-night rawness of his Hamburg days, but the voice remains unmistakably his and no one can accuse him of going all mid-Atlantic. Meanwhile, there is some musical interplay with the vocals, but whether it is Les Harvey emulating a trumpet on his guitar or trumpeters Bud Parkes and Derek Watkins doing the opposite is hard to tell.

'Midnight Moses' is not only the best song on this album, but it also remains one of the best in Harvey's long, storied career, and he was absolutely right to recycle it with SAHB. It would have been criminal for it to be lost on this all-but-forgotten album.

'Hello L.A., Bye Bye Birmingham' (Delaney Bramlett, Mac Davis)
Co-writer Mac Davis is best known for the hits he wrote for Elvis Presley, including 'In the Ghetto' and 'A Little Less Conversation', while Bramlett enjoyed success in the duo Delaney & Bonnie. Several acts recorded this song as the Sixties came to a close, including Nancy Sinatra and Blue Cheer, but Harvey's version was first on the market. This features a tremendous arrangement by *Hair* band regulars Derek Wardsworth and Frank Ricotti which combines Memphis soul with Nashville fingerpicking.

'Broken Hearted Fairytale' (Harvey, Andy McMaster)
Some more Nashville vibes, but this time sounding as if played by a minstrel beamed in from Tudor England and coloured by the toy town sounds much favoured by British dabblers in late-Sixties psychedelia. This runs the risk of making it sound more exciting than it actually is, but this mid-tempo tune isn't particularly memorable, despite being co-written by Andy McMaster, who, as a member of The Motors, later had a hand in such irrepressible hits as 'Dancing the Night Away', 'Airport', and 'Forget About You'.

'Donna' (James Rado, Gerome Ragni, Galt MacDermot)
The 5th Dimension created their signature song by making a medley from two *Hair* songs, 'Aquarius' and 'Let the Sunshine In'; it also topped the US and Canadian charts and went top ten around the world. By combining another two songs from the musical, 'Ain't Got No' with 'I Got Life', Nina Simone also found herself with a brand-new signature piece, and a UK number two hit to boot. Alex Harvey took a fifth song from Hair, the Fifties pastiche 'Donna', and, well, did nothing with it, really. Perhaps he was too close to the material, having performed it most nights for over a year by the time he recorded it. Or perhaps 'Donna' just isn't that good a song.

'Roman Wall Blues' (W. H. Auden, Harvey)
It's one of those co-writing credits that makes you look twice, like that time Christina Rossetti hunkered down with Gustav Holst to knock out cheerless

festive favourite 'In the Bleak Midwinter'. Alex Harvey and... W. H. Auden? Surely that can't be right?

Happily, it is, because, as with that Rosetti-Holst collaboration, it is a case of a later musician adapting the words of an earlier poet. 'Roman Wall Blues' tells of a Roman soldier manning the titular wall while questioning what he is even doing there and fretting about what's going on with his girlfriend back home, especially since 'Aulus goes hanging around her place'. Harvey sets the poem to the one-step-removed-from-blues prog common to the late '60s (see Deep Purple, Jethro Tull, and even future SAHB members Tear Gas), but in doing so creates an atmospheric soundscape with a vaguely middle eastern coda.

'Jumping Jack Flash' (Mick Jagger, Keith Richards)

Hair had several innovative features, not least that the cast could do whatever they wanted on stage when they were not involved in any given scene so long as they didn't distract from those who were, and that the band concluded the evening by playing whatever they wanted, including their own songs and covers. This cover, a straightforward reading of the Stones' original if not for the pumped-up brass section, was a regular inclusion.

'Hammer Song' (Harvey)

This is a slightly more up-tempo yet oddly less energetic version of another future favourite from *Framed*. While not in the same league as 'Midnight Moses', it is strong enough to understand why Harvey would want to save it from obscurity.

'Let My Bluebird Sing' (Harvey)

A positively jaunty song with some laid-back blues guitar, presumably by brother Les, 'Let My Bluebird Sing' also features a fine vocal from Alex and a wonderfully dissonant middle eight where the piano is used as a percussive instrument. A blues song for people that don't like blues songs.

'Maxine' (June Foray)

As with the rest of the album 'Maxine' boasts an excellent brass arrangement, but even this can't disguise the fact that this mid-tempo, mildly moribund melodrama is precisely the type of song Scott Walker would have sung on a long-wiped, late-Sixties Saturday night light entertainment show.

'(Down at) Bart's Place' (Harvey)

This is a disposable instrumental that combines then-outdated Merseybeat with Stax soul.

'Candy' (Harvey)

'Candy' is an exuberant little album closer that clocks in at under three minutes. Despite the singalong quality of the vocal melody, this song serves as a better showcase for the musicianship of the band than the previous instrumental did.

Related Songs
'The Sunday Song' (Harvey)
'All kinds of people were a-holding hands/Dancin' through the flowers to the promised lands'. As you can tell from that opening couplet, 1967 has arrived, and Harvey embraces the zeitgeist by forming the psychedelic band Giant Moth. Decca must have believed the Alex Harvey name carried more weight, however, and released this single under his name alone.

Like contemporaneous releases by the Small Faces and The Move, this is a perfectly hummable blend of pop and psychedelia, but unfortunately, it stiffed. It deserved better and it is possible Decca called it wrong; 'The Sunday Song' might have gained some airplay if released under the Giant Moth moniker, thus presenting it as something new – which it was – rather than yet another song by the Glaswegian that had been knocking on pop's door for the better part of a decade.

Syd Barrett reviewed 'Sunday Song' for *Melody Maker*: 'Nice sounds, yeah. Wow. It moved me a little bit' – knock yourself out, Syd – 'but I don't think it will be a hit'.

'Horizons' (A. Harvey, L. Harvey)
It might be less poppy than the lead track, but this flipside of 'The Sunday Song' was strong enough to earn its own A-side. The flute and the flanging establish its psych credentials, and while it might not be in the same league as 'Strawberry Fields Forever/Penny Lane', this 45 is nonetheless a perfect snapshot of the days when London swung.

'Maybe Someday' (Heron)
The slow start suggests Giant Moth are taking the Incredible String Band's 'Maybe Someday' in a different direction, but they soon revert to the jaunty pace of the original. However, they opt for a folk-rock arrangement rather than the pure folk approach adopted by the ISB. This cover demonstrates Harvey has temporarily abandoned his habit of exhuming songs from previous decades and generations and seeks inspiration from the then-current music scene, but while an astute choice, it pales compared to the previous 45.

'Curtains For My Baby' (Harvey)
Spoke too soon! This might be an original, but Harvey is once again raking over dem blues with a touch of New Orleans jazz thrown in free of charge. The Beatles and The Kinks were also adapting old music styles in 1967, but whereas they took their inspiration from British music hall, Harvey was still fixated on the USA. 'Curtains For My Baby' isn't a bad song and it would have fitted nicely on any of Alex's previous long players (or, for that matter, future

ones), but here it is the wrong sound at the wrong time and is the weakest of the Giant Moth cuts.

Hair Rave-Up (1969)

The sleeve notes of this album remind us that 'There is no final curtain to the show, so the swingiest cast of all time invite you to join them on stage at the Shaftesbury Theatre for what has become widely known as the Hair Rave-Up'. This album does not document one of those post-show stage invasions, but rather a one-off gig that took place before a specially invited audience and comprises a selection of songs that regularly featured in the 'Hair Rave-Up', including a couple of tracks from the musical itself. Harvey takes control of the microphone for four tracks produced by Cyril Stapleton.

'Hair' (Galt MacDermot, James Rado, Gerome Ragni)

The first is the musical's title track, normally performed by the entire cast with solo spots for Paul Nicholas and Oliver Tobias. Harvey effortlessly makes the song his own, even allowing his inner Glaswegian to emerge ever so slightly, a nod to his future vocal direction. The Hairband are as flawless here as they were throughout *Roman Wall Blues*, resulting in a reading of 'Hair' that is nothing short of thrilling.

'Royal International Love-In' (Alex Harvey, Steve Stevenson)

Co-written with US jazz saxophonist Stevenson, this is a fun, if forgettable, Fifties rocker taken down from the shelf, dusted, and given a Swinging Sixties title. The song's rapid pace allows Harvey to coax out his consonant-crunching future voice that bit more.

'Bond Street Baby' (Alex Harvey)

While the melody of this Harvey original may not be memorable, or even present, 'Bond Street Baby' should at least be remembered as the song in which Alex fully let his Glaswegian accent run riot. Rock's most quietly menacing voice had arrived.

'Birthday' (John Lennon, Paul McCartney)

This is a too-faithful reading of the *White Album* Beatles song, and therefore offers nothing new, but would no doubt have had them rockin' in the aisles at the Rave-In.

Rock Workshop (1970)

Rock Workshop were the blandly named jazz-fusion rock ensemble founded by guitarist Ray Russell. They released two worthwhile albums, the eponymous debut in 1970 and *The Very Last Time* the following year, both of which came and went without fanfare. Although the CD release of *The Very Last Time* features Harvey on the bonus tracks, these were just alternate versions of songs he sang on the first album and are not reviewed here. Harvey recorded his vocals for the first album on 4-5 April 1970, and it was released in August.

'Ice Cold' (Ray Russell, R. Shepherd)

This is a strong track, a big brassy affair that sounds like Blood, Sweat and Tears fronted by Van Morrison. Harvey may have temporarily put his Glaswegian accent back in the box, but that doesn't deter him from delivering a powerful vocal.

'You To Lose' (Roy Cameron, Ray Russell)

In between an overwrought introduction and a twittering conclusion, the various members of Rock Workshop demonstrate what brilliant musicians they are, but no one remembered to bring along a tune.

'Hole in Her Stocking' (Alex Harvey, Ray Russell)

Warning: sacrilege ahead! This raucous reading of the song that would reappear on *Framed* is far superior to the Sensational Alex Harvey Band version. The brass section is so punchy they threaten to burst through the speakers, there is a wonderfully discordant middle-eight, and, unlike the more well-known version, the original doesn't overstay its welcome.

'Wade in the Water' (Traditional, arranged Alex Harvey, Ray Russell)

'Wade in the Water' has an interesting history, in that it started life as an African American spiritual, was a code song associated with the Underground Railroad, and became an anthem of the civil rights movement courtesy of the Staples Singers. Jazz pianist Ramsey Lewis had the most commercially successful version when he took his instrumental reading of the song to number 19 in the US pop charts in 1966. Unfortunately, Harvey kills it here, and not in a good way, choosing to dig his SAHB-style vocals out the box when he should have gone for something more soulful. That the band are so blisteringly brilliant only further exposes Alex as the weakest link.

'Born in the City' (Alex Harvey, Ray Russell)

After an 'experimental' opening that no one needs to hear twice, this song settles into a solid jazz-soul groove with a ragged Harvey growl voicing the perfunctory lyrics.

Piggy Go Getter – Tear Gas

Personnel:
David Batchelor: vocals
Zal Cleminson: acoustic and electric guitar, vocals
Eddie Campbell: organ, piano, vocals
Chris Glen: bass guitar, vocals
Wullie Munro: drums, tambourine, maracas, Chinese finger cymbals, vocals
Produced at Regent Sound Studios, London, by Tony Chapman
Release Date: October 1970
Label: Famous Music
Highest Chart Place: Did not chart
Running time: 35:40

While Alex is happily whiling away his time in the *Hair* orchestra pit and taking the sporadic foray into recording, it is time to meet the men that would put the B in SAHB.

Chris Glen, the future Harvey Band's bass-wielding, jockstrap-wearing boy blue, was born November 1950 in Paisley, Renfrewshire. Glen opted for a career in music after working briefly as a quantity surveyor, and immediately selected the bass guitar as his instrument of choice. By the late Sixties, he was playing in a band called Jade, notable as it included not just Glen but also singer Jim Diamond, who would go on to enjoy chart success both as a member of PhD and as a solo artist, and lead guitarist Jim Lacey, who would later join the Alan Bown Set. Despite regular gigging in London and a Scottish tour supporting The Move, Jade failed to make an impact. Glen jumped ship when he was offered a place in a band called Mustard.

Mustard emerged from the ashes of a previous band called the Bo Weavils, who named themselves after a beetle and, like The Beatles, replaced the second 'e' with an 'a'. The Weavils were formed by schoolfriends George Gilmour (vocals), Alistair Cleminson (lead guitar), David Batchelor (rhythm guitar, later keyboards), Ricky Archibald (bass), and Jimmy Brand (drums). Despite their tender years, the band quickly made an impact on Scotland's burgeoning independent music scene, and, according to Martin Kielty, author of *SAHB Story: The Tale of the Sensational Alex Harvey Band*, soon joined the Poets, the Beatstalkers, and the Pathfinders as one of the country's 'Big Four'. The Beatles, the Stones, the Small Faces and the like may have dominated the charts just as they did in England, but these homegrown bands strode the live circuit north of the border like Caledonian colossi.

The Beatstalkers, for example, were regularly billed as 'Scotland's Top Group'. Probably the best illustration of how big this band were was an event to launch their new single that took place at Glasgow's 1,800-capacity Dennistoun Palais, which they managed to sell out despite the Beatstalkers being in London. Appearing in their stead were five life-size cardboard cut-outs, while singer Davie Lennox said hello to the audience over the telephone after which the DJ played the new song. It was, in essence, a low-tech version of the virtual concert, decades before Kraftwerk or Abba came up with the concept. Among the Beatstalkers not appearing that night was one Eddie Campbell, who we will meet again shortly.

The support act at this event, meanwhile, were the Bo Weavils, who, unlike the headliners, appeared live. According to a retrospective piece written by music journalist Russell Leadbetter in *The Herald*, the Weavils, who specialised in Motown and R&B, honed their craft and built their following at this same venue, before progressing to conquer dancehalls and clubs across Scotland. Such was the band's rising popularity that pop columnist Gordon Buchanan declared in a 1965 edition of *The Evening Times* that the Bo-Weavils 'will be bigger than The Beatstalkers', prompting 2,000 female fans of the latter to send a petition to the newspaper protesting Buchanan's temerity.

However, a mark of true success for a Scottish band was to make it in London, and while some did, such as Dean Ford and the Gaylords under their new guise as the Marmalade, most, including all of 'the Big Four' did not. The closest to do so were The Poets, who managed one solitary breach of the UK Top Forty when their single 'Now We're Thru' reached 31.

The times were truly a-changin' as the Sixties wore on, and albums such as *Sgt Pepper's Lonely Hearts Club Band*, *The Piper at the Gates of Dawn*, and *Are You Experienced* were introducing new genres in the shape of psychedelia, progressive rock, and heavy/hard rock. Equally importantly, they were ushering in the era of the album. Cleminson and Batchelor decided that was where they wanted to be, so they formed a new group called Mustard, soon rebranded as Tear Gas.

A few faces came and went before Tear Gas's line-up settled on Cleminson and Batchelor (guitar and vocals, respectively) and Chris Glen from Jade on bass. Joining them was drummer Richard 'Wullie' Munro, who had been in Ritchie Blackmore's brief pre-Purple group Mandrake Root, and Eddie Campbell on keyboards. Like Cleminson and Batchelor, the former Beatstalker had grown frustrated by his band's inability to make a dent in England, this despite a young David Bowie writing some of their songs and even providing backing vocals and guitar on 'Silver Tree Top School for Boys'. When their van and equipment was stolen in 1969, The Beatstalkers gave up the ghost and Campbell immediately hooked up with Tear Gas.

The new band continued to cover Motown songs at their concerts, but these were now interspersed with heavier covers such as Steppenwolf's 'Born to be Wild', 'Love Story' by Jethro Tull, and 'Black Night' by Deep Purple. Eddie Tobin, a friend of the band who would later manage Billy Connolly, SAHB, Nazareth, and Glasgow's famed Apollo Theatre, signed on as manager, and the band got to work on original material. Tobin soon secured them a deal with Famous Music, an unusual choice of label as it was originally formed to release songs from movies made by Paramount Pictures. Over the decades, Famous has had hits – and Oscar winners – with songs such as 'Thanks for the Memories' (*The Big Broadcast of 1938*), 'Mona Lisa' (*Captain Carey, U.S.A*), 'Moon River' (*Breakfast at Tiffany's*), 'Where Do I Begin' (*Love Story*), and, more recently, 'Up Where We Belong' from *An Officer and A Gentleman* and 'My Heart Will Go On' from *Titanic*. It seems an unlikely home for a Glaswegian band with prog and hard rock tendencies, but as Cleminson says in the sleeve notes for the 2019 reissue of Tear Gas's debut album *Piggy Go Getter*: 'For us, it was a dream come true. Not just becoming a signed band, but also getting the chance to go to London to record the first album. That was amazing'.

Cleminson remembers drummer Munro coming up with the curious album title while under the influence of acid, whereas Glen recalls it spinning out of the use of the word 'pig' as a derogatory term for both women and the police. Regardless of its origins, it is as memorable as it is meaningless. No expense was spared on the design of the original record sleeve, which featured a textured cover and two cartoon strips by Brian Engel informing the reader of Tear Gas's views on the English and the police; 'Thurs a lo a' skinheids in Inglan noo'adays' and 'Wi'oot a doot, Bri'ish police arra best in ra wurruld' are just two of the nuggets of wisdom contained therein. *Piggy Go Getter* was produced by Tony Chapman, an early associate of the Rolling Stones and former member of The Herd.

Just prior to the album's release, Al Cleminson became Zal Cleminson, the alteration suggested by Davey Batchelor, who, possibly inspired by the Lovin' Spoonful's Zal Yanovsky, thought that it sounded cool.

Piggy Go Getter is a very uneven album, its many musical styles less a band comfortable with diversity, as SAHB would be, but rather one not yet sure of its own identity. With the exceptions of 'Nothing Can Change Your Mind' and 'Big House' none of the tunes possess the burrowing power of an earworm. More crucially, by the time it was released in October 1970, *Piggy Go Getter* already sounded old; while *Black Sabbath* and *Deep Purple in Rock* forge exciting new sounds for the 1970s, Tear Gas sound like a band trapped in the amber of the Sixties. Unfortunately, John Q. Public thought the same way, and the album only shifted about 5,000 upon initial release.

'Lost Awakening' (Batcheler, Cleminson)

The verses of 'Lost Awakening', a bog-standard tale of love lost, are largely voice and acoustic guitar affairs with occasional skittery electric embellishment, the remaining players content to wait to the chorus before kicking in. At the middle eight, someone stumbles upon a cupboard full of wah-wah pedals, and what had been merely pleasant now belatedly grabs the attention as any good album opener should, as the vague Deep Purple mark one vibes suddenly morph into the soundtrack to some Blaxploitation flick. That last sentence runs the risk of making 'Lost Awakening' sound more exciting on paper than it is on vinyl, but it is a solid, if not spectacular, start to a new band's debut album.

'Your Woman's Gone and Left You' (Batcheler, Cleminson)
If the lyrics are to be believed, women were clearly quite feckless as the
Seventies dawned, to the extent that if their partner was away from home
for any length of time then they would simply leave and find another one.
Or maybe they moved out because they had enough of bell-bottomed
misogynists treating them as property, as indicated in the possessive title.
Either way, this starts like it might be Lindisfarne before quickly becoming
meandering and unmemorable. There is a nice echo effect used on the vocal,
but unfortunately, it is right at the end, and the song fades just as you sit up
and take notice.

'Night Girl' (Batcheler, Cleminson, Glen)
As a live act, Tear Gas had a reputation for being offputtingly loud, resulting
in them acquiring the nickname Fear Gas. Three songs in, and none of that
ferocity is evident on *Piggy Go Getter*. 'Night Girl' is not dissimilar to 'Lost
Awakening' in that it favours acoustic verses followed by choruses that rock,
but not too hard, and like the opener, this track is pleasant without ever
threatening to knock anyone's socks off. It does, however, feature a double-
tracked solo from Cleminson, and some wintery 'Na-na-na-ing' that wouldn't
sound out of place on a 5th Dimension album. Alternatively, think Blood,
Sweat and Tears without the section. Nice song.

'Nothing Can Change Your Mind' (Batcheler, Cleminson)
A distant cousin of Marmalade's contemporaneous hit 'Reflections Of My
Life', this is the poppiest track on the album thus far, and comes complete
with a catchy, singalong chorus with some nice harmonising. A single that
never was.

'Living for Today' (Batcheler, Cleminson)
A catchy chorus features here too, but the Purple mark one vibes are no
longer vague on the verses between, as Davey Batchelor, Eddie Campbell, and
Chris Glen do *New Faces*-winning impersonations (or *Britain's Got Talent*-
winning, for those of you joining us in the 21st century) of Rod Evans, Jon
Lord, and Nick Simper respectively.

'Big House' (Batcheler, Cleminson)
More poppiness, this time with a distinct country and western twang, thanks
to the honky-tonk piano and slide guitar. The music may be influenced by
Nashville, but the harmonies are pure west coast, even if Batchelor's lead
vocals don't stretch any further than Girvan.

'Mirrors of Sorrow' (Batcheler, Cleminson, Glen)
One would expect a title like 'Mirrors of Sorrow' to come with a prog song
attached, and huzzah, one would not be disappointed. This also comes with

a sprinkling of late-Sixties British bluesiness, and a soupçon of psych. Where it departs from prog norms is the running time; this clocks in at under three minutes, and that includes a clever false fade.

'Look What Else is Happening' (Batcheler, Cleminson, Glen)

Track eight stays in psych rock territory and was presumably the number that was used to showcase the individual players' talents when performed live. It opens with a drum solo from Wullie Munro, who is soon joined and ably supported by Chris Glen, while the mid-section allows both Cleminson and Campbell to strut their respective stuff.

'I'm Fallin' Far Behind' (Batcheler, Cleminson, Munro)

The penultimate song dabbles in the white soul that would later propel the Average White Band to US superstardom, with a fat funky bassline serving as the tune's foundation.

'Witches Come Today' (Batcheler, Cleminson)

The concluding track is the album's heaviest, and although also sounding indebted to the first three Purple albums, it also hints at things to come. One of *Piggy Go Getter*'s best.

Tear Gas – Tear Gas

Personnel:
Davey Batchelor: vocals and guitar
Zal Cleminson: lead guitar
Chris Glen: bass
Ted McKenna (credited as Eddie McKenna): drums
Produced at Intersound and Island Studios, London, by Tony Chapman
Release Date: August 1971
Label: Regal Zonophone
Highest Chart Place: Did not chart
Running time: 48:49

Wullie Munro elected to leave Tear Gas after *Piggy Go Getter*, forming the brilliantly named Berserk Crocodile with former Dream Police members Hamish Stuart and Matt Irvine and ex-Poet Fraser Watson. The Crocodiles failed to make a splash, but all bar Munro went on to enjoy a career in music, with Hamish Stuart finding most success as a founding member of the Average White Band and later sideman to both Chaka Khan and Paul McCartney. Meanwhile, another former Dream Policeman, Ted McKenna, replaced Munro behind the Tear Gas drumkit. Eddie Campbell bailed shortly after work began on the second album, and the remaining foursome elected to be a guitar-driven group that would rely on session musicians for any keyboard parts.

Eddie Tobin got the band a new record deal, this time with Regal Zonophone, then home to progressive acts such as Procol Harum, Tyrannosaurus Rex, Joe Cocker, and the Move, and therefore a more natural home for Tear Gas than Famous Music had been. Tony Chapman remained on board as producer.

Hipgnosis, the hip design studio that had made their name designing Pink Floyd covers from *A Saucerful of Secrets* on, came up with the album cover. According to Glen, the cover concept of an explosion emanating from a hand was his, but it was Hipgnosis's Storm Thorgerson who came up with the idea of using an egg being crushed to represent the blast.

Tear Gas is a stronger effort than the debut, thanks to a superior production job, stronger songwriting, and, more significantly, the band developing a clearer understanding of their identity and musical genre. According to Cleminson and Glen, their sophomore effort also outperformed its predecessor in terms of sales, so while it didn't set the world alight, creative and commercial progress was being made. So, naturally, it was at this point Tear Gas decided to call it a day. Dave Batchelor had never set out to be a frontman and had no desire to continue. His preference was to work behind the scenes in some sound engineering or production capacity. Cleminson succinctly summed up the split: 'The second album was a step in the right direction for me personally, but Dave himself realised he wasn't the right singer for the job. Without which we couldn't progress'.

Any dreams the band members harboured of Tear Gas joining Purple, Sabbath, and Zeppelin in rock's upper echelons were now in tatters, the band enlisting instead in the School of Rock Also-Rans alongside fellow early Seventies stalwarts such as Warhorse and Captain Beyond. That might sound like the Tear Gas story ends in a major downer, but what the band members did next would of course prove to be nothing short of sensational.

'That's What's Real' (Batchelor, Cleminson)

If *Piggy Go Getter* was influenced by the original Purple line-up, then 'That's What's Real' suggests this new iteration of Tear Gas had been listening to *Deep Purple In Rock*. Out go the psych and prog elements, out too the lingering scent of the Sixties, and in come stabbing guitar riffs, a beefed-up pulsing bassline, and drums muffled like distant thunder. And while Ian Gillan's passaggio breaks or Dan McCafferty's paint-stripping upper register are out of Davey Batchelor's range, he sounds far more assured here than he did on any song on the band's debut.

As with the *Piggy* songs, 'That's What Real' lacks a killer hook, but on this evidence, Tear Gas are now truly a hard rock band, and kudos are deserved for the surprise ending.

'Love Story' (Ian Anderson)

The golden rule of cover versions is to make it your own while honouring the original, and that's exactly what The Gas (as precisely no one ever called them) do here with their take on Jethro Tull's 1968 singles chart debut. Tear Gas's first major alteration is to take their time in building the song up, so that much of the first two and a half minutes is very sparse, often just voice, guitar, and ominously sustained bass note. On approaching the 2.40 mark, the song explodes into a hard and fast bluesy rocker, more Zeppelin than Tull, with Cleminson cutting loose with two blistering solos.

'Love Story' was a regular fixture in the band's setlist, often as the opening number, and they obviously maintained their love of the song as they revisited it as the Sensational Alex Harvey Band on 1976's *The Penthouse Tapes*.

'Lay It On Me' (Batchelor, Cleminson)

This has some scintillating slide guitar from Cleminson, and Batchelor's voice sounds comfortably at home, but there is no escaping that this is a fairly routine slab of bar room boogie.

There is some confusion as to who played the piano on this track. In *The Bass Business*, Chris Glen credits Hugh McKenna, while in the liner notes of the 2019 release *Tear Gas*, Cleminson names Ronnie Leahy as the ivory tinkler. Leahy would join Glen and Cleminson in the Sensational Party Boys in the 1990s (having previously played with Zal in the short-lived Tandoori Cassette), before becoming a member of Nazareth between 1994 and 2002.

'Woman for Sale' (Batchelor, Cleminson)
'Woman for Sale' is a strong track, possibly the album's strongest, with a memorable, crunching guitar riff along the lines of a less muddy Tony Iommi. Cleminson's emergence as axe hero continues with some fine six-string pyrotechnics at the end. Batchelor nails the vocal, his voice clear and high in the mix, and he is supported by strong backing vocals on the chorus.

'I'm Glad' (Batchelor, Cleminson)
This is a song where the sum is most definitely not greater than the parts. The main riff anticipates a handful of Kiss songs, 1977's 'All-American Man' being the first to spring to mind, after which a time change leads to a lengthy middle eight elevated by some top-drawer soloing from Cleminson, then a further change introduces a brief British bluesy ballad, before the song returns to the original riff. These elements just about work while the disc is spinning, but remembering the melody upon the song's conclusion is a challenge.

'Where is My Answer' (Batchelor, Cleminson)
This is almost a companion piece to 'Witches Come Today' from *Piggy Go Getter*, in that whereas that song hinted at the direction the band would take in the future, this song, with its returning echoes of Purple mark one, recalls the style Tear Gas adopted on their debut. That said, this ballad rocks heavy at the chorus, and is, therefore, equally at home on this record.

'Jailhouse Rock'/'All Shook Up' (Jerry Leiber, Mike Stoller/Otis Blackwell, Elvis Presley)
This medley of old Elvis hits was the first track recorded for *Tear Gas* and was made when Eddie Campbell was still in the band. The inspiration was less the King and more Jeff Beck, who had recorded the two songs on his second album *Beck-Ola* (1969), which was also the first credited to the Jeff Beck Group. Commenting on this medley on the sleeve notes to the 2019 reissue of *Tear Gas*, Cleminson says:

> That was something that Beck and his band had done on their *Beck-Ola* album. I wanted to see if we could play this in the same way as he did. So, what we did is directly copy the arrangement they'd used. I make no bones about it; we did steal what the Jeff Beck Group had done.

Regardless of its inspiration, this can't conceal the primitivism of the source material and is the least interesting entry in Tear Gas's short recording career. It is also hampered by Batchelor's voice being buried too deep in the mix, and by the fact he is no Rod Stewart.

'The First Time' (Batchelor, Cleminson)

Unfortunately, the band follow the Elvis medley with their slightest composition to date. 'The First Time' strains to be epic but has to settle for meandering, resulting in the album concluding in disappointing style.

The Joker is Wild – Alex Harvey

Personnel:
Alex Harvey: vocals and guitar
Leslie Harvey: guitar
Pete Kelly: piano
Jim Condron: bass guitar
George Butler: drums
Stephen Allan: engineer, synthesiser, sound effects on 'Flying Saucer's Daughter'
Produced at Philips (Phonogram) Studio, London, by Paul Murphy
Release Date: 1972
Label: Metronome Records
Highest Chart Place: Did not chart
Running time: 38:51

Before getting to the point where Alex Harvey and Tear Gas meet, we have
The Joker is Wild, an album rarely mentioned in Harvey biographies, perhaps
because it isn't considered 'canon'. Aided by brother Leslie and two of his
Giant Moth bandmates, amongst others, Harvey reputedly only lay down his
vocal tracks as a guide for one Tony Caldeira, who wrote the title track and
'Silhouette and Shadow'. Caldeira promptly failed to materialise, and Harvey's
cheque for the session bounced into the bargain. It's a grand tale, but the
presence of Frank Zappa's 'Willie the Pimp', 'Hare Krishna' from *Hair*, and
Harvey perennials 'Penicillin Blues' and 'Make Love to You' all indicate that the
singer had greater involvement than the accepted 'origin' story suggests. What
is undeniable is that producer Paul Murphy, who had produced the two Soul
Band albums, sold the tapes to Swedish record label Metronome, who released
it under the *Joker is Wild* moniker. Following SAHB's success, Metronome
shamelessly re-released this with the new title *This Is The Sensational Alex
Harvey Band*. Photos of Zal and company even adorned the front and
back covers despite the fact SAHB didn't even exist when this album was
recorded. Ultimately, the overall sound of *The Joker is Wild* is that of a band
rehearsing in the studio, a curio of interest only to the most dedicated Harvey
fan. Sensational, it is not. According to Jon Tiven of *Circus Raves* magazine
(December 1974), Harvey himself dismissed the album as 'a heap of mush'.

Leslie Harvey had by now appeared on several of his brother's albums, but
he had also forged his own career with proggy blues rockers Stone the Crows,
who had three albums to their name and were looked after by Led Zeppelin's
heavyweight manager Peter Grant. There was a sense that the Crows could take
off, but it ended in tragedy on 3 May 1972 when Les Harvey was electrocuted
onstage at the Top Rank Bingo Club in Swansea. Talking to *Mojo* in 2000,
Maggie Bell, Harvey's partner in both the band and life, recalled: 'It was a
concert for doctors and nurses. I remember Leslie saying, 'There's something
wrong here, but we want this to be a good gig, so bear with us for a moment'.
He put his hand on the mike, and he was gone. It was just as quick as that'.

Leslie's death also tolled the bell for Stone the Crows. They released one more album, *Ontinuous Performance*, most of which had been recorded with Leslie, and recruited another talented young Scottish guitarist Jimmy McCulloch for the remaining tracks. They split up following the tour to support the album.

Alex was naturally devastated by his brother's death and was, at times, inconsolable. But losing Les also gave him a renewed determination to succeed. It was almost as if Alex was content being a working musician while Stone the Crows looked poised to break through, but with Les gone Alex was determined the remaining Harvey brother would succeed in the name of both. Easier said than done, of course. It was now fifteen years since he had won the Scotland's Tommy Steele contest and hadn't appreciably moved forward any since then, despite having released several albums and gigged incessantly. In the meantime, Hamburg contemporaries The Beatles had been, gone, and had changed popular music forever, and even David Bowie, the young man with whom he had swapped science fiction books in the Sixties, appeared to be on the verge of something big.

In an industry that prized youth and success, 37-year-old Alex Harvey had neither, and his daring new two-point action plan didn't sound particularly promising: (a) Find a backing band that is good, and (b) find a backing band that is Scottish.

'The Joker is Wild' (Tony Caldeira)

Harvey delivers a shouty vocal with poor enunciation, a strange approach to what was ostensibly meant to be a vocal guide, especially considering the man could sing when he wanted to. As for the song, although credited to Tony Caldeira, it sounds suspiciously like something Harvey would have written after playing the *Hair* songs for three straight years. Caldeira increasingly sounds like a non-existent character.

'Penicillin Blues' (Harvey)

Here's Harvey's second stab at 'Penicillin Blues', the first appearing on the abandoned second Soul Band album, and as with that previous effort, the album credits fail to acknowledge original composers, Brownie McGhee and Sonny Terry; Harvey presumably gets the nod for his lyrical ad-libbing. This version contains some clever syncopation from drummer George Butler but overall lacks the musical sophistication of the Soul Band's version. Les Harvey would revisit the song with Stone the Crows, and it would appear on their *Ontinuous Performance* album, released after the guitarist's death.

'Make Love to You' (Harvey)

Also inexplicably credited to Harvey on the original sleeve, this is simply a slightly retitled, reworked version of the Willie Dixon song Alex previously covered on the 1964 *Alex Harvey and His Soul Band* album.

'I'm Just a Man' (Larry Santos)
This is a relatively faithful reading of the title track of the debut album by smoothy white soulster Larry Santos, and punts Harvey dangerously close to that MOR territory that manager, David Firmstone, so wanted him to occupy.

'He Ain't Heavy, He's My Brother' (Bob Scott, Bob Russell)
Perhaps it is the gloomy bassline that suckers Harvey into singing lower than his range, but he soon recovers, if performing the Hollies classic with all the panache of a Paisley pub singer can be called a recovery. This is another blatant attempt at launching Harvey as a singer in the Tom Jones/Englebert Humperdinck mould. The road is long, but never more so than in this version of the song.

'Silhouette and Shadow' (Tony Caldeira)
This opens with a scuzzy, Sabbath-esque intro that then decides to hang around for the entirety of the song, over which Alex narrates rather than sings some nonsense about the silhouette being an impression of a shadow or some such. On the plus side, it hits the fade upon the two-minute mark.

'Hare Krishna'/'Willie the Pimp' (Frank Zappa)
The bulk of this track – over eight whopping minutes! – is occupied by a performance of 'Hare Krishna' from *Hair* that would have sounded hopelessly outdated in 1972, what with the Sanskrit mantra, the channel-hopping sitar, and Harvey singing as if undergoing primal scream therapy. It then jumps onto Zappa's 'Willie the Pimp', which drops the Eastern affectations without discernibly altering the listening experience. Like 'Highlands' from Dylan's *Time Out of Mind* album, this need never be listened to more than once, and the singing technique only reinforces the impression that the vocal guides story was a classic case of Harvey mythologising.

'Flying Saucer's Daughter' (Harvey, Paul Murphy)
Another five years too late number. Despite the vaguely glammy title, this sounds as if it was lifted from a 24-Hour Happening at the UFO Club or Middle-Earth, circa 1967. The fate of 'Tony Caldeira', meanwhile, remains unknown.

Framed – The Sensational Alex Harvey Band

Personnel:
Alex Harvey: vocals
Zal Cleminson: lead guitar
Hugh McKenna: electric piano
Chris Glen: bass guitar
Ted McKenna (credited as Eddie McKenna): drums
Phil Kenzie: tenor saxophone
Big Bud's Brass (likely Bud Parkes, Martin Drover, Phil Kenzie, Dave Coxhill, Geoff Driscoll): brass section
Produced at Morgan Studios, London, by the Sensational Alex Harvey Band
Release Date: December 1972
Label: Vertigo
Highest Chart Place: Did not chart
Running time: 42:09

The three remaining members of Tear Gas – Zal Cleminson, Chris Glen, Ted McKenna – were unsure of how to proceed. They were short a frontman and singer, and the decision not to enlist a keyboard player for the second album was now regarded as a mistake. This second problem had an easy fix, as Ted's cousin Hugh McKenna was pressed into service. Hugh was a somewhat reluctant recruit who, by his own admission, didn't particularly like Tear Gas's brand of hard rock, or indeed hard rock at all, preferring instead the likes of Elton John and Joni Mitchell. Here's a summary of Hugh's musical journey to 1972 courtesy of his old bandmate and lifelong friend Owen Mullen:

Hugh and I met in our first year at St. Patrick's High School in Coatbridge, and he introduced me to this big gangly guy called Ted, who was then called Eddie. Hugh's family were very much a musical family – Hugh's mum and dad were both 'on the boards', with his dad being an accordionist on the variety circuit for decades. His mother was a singer and Hugh's sister Mae inherited the genes and became a very successful session singer, working with the likes of Kylie Minogue and Michael Jackson. So, Hugh was always going to go into music.

Hugh and me and Ted became a gang of three, inseparable and – now that I think about it – probably insufferable too! 'The Clique de la Clique', Ted called us. Our first band was The Vibrations. Hugh didn't have a keyboard, so only Ted was in it at this point, but Hugh later got an old electric piano and we started to rehearse in Ted's bedroom on Friday nights, and during the week in class, we'd be singing harmonies rather than learning whatever the teachers were trying to put in our heads. Then they left to join a band called The Rare Breed, and pretty quickly, they got me and Vibrations singer Jim Coventry in there too. We played all over the country, mostly Tamla stuff.

51

We changed our name to Bubbles, bought a transit van and went professional on 12 September 1969. We did five live BBC Radio shows and tons of gigs, even a couple of tours down south, playing places like Carlisle, Sheffield, Warrington, and Manchester (where we went to Old Trafford and saw Denis Law and Bobby Charlton beat Huddersfield Town 1 – 0, with the goal from George Best). To be honest, we were pretty good. Great harmonies from Hugh and I, although it was Hugh and Ted who were the natural players.

The line-up of Hugh, Ted, Jim, Tom Wigfield and I lasted about two years. In the end, Ted left when Hamish Stuart asked him to join the Dream Police, and Hugh left after he and I had a falling out in Edinburgh one night, although we stayed friends and met frequently.

Zal, Chris, and Ted now had their keyboard player, so all that was required to start anew was a singer. Fortunately, there was a guy in London on the lookout for a team of top players, preferably Scottish. Even more fortunately, there was a self-made millionaire and dabbler in music promotion who believed the London guy had star potential and just needed the right band. In other words, re-enter Bill Fehilly. Since his days as housepainter in the atomic city and highland café owner, Fehilly had grown an empire of bingo halls the length and breadth of the country and was now willing to invest in one last hurrah to make a star out of old friend Alex Harvey. One of Fehilly's contacts was Eddie Tobin, who had managed Tear Gas, and who now informed Bill that the band were currently rudderless and in need of a frontman.

Harvey went up to Glasgow to check out this outfit, unaware they had earlier supported him in February that year at the Marquee and were less than impressed. However, the belief was that Tear Gas had run its course, so they had nothing to lose by hooking up with Harvey to see how things went. They met at the Burns Howff bar in the city centre before moving on to Thor Studios to run through some songs, including 'Framed' and 'I Just Want To Make Love to You'. The one that sealed the deal, however, was 'Midnight Moses'. Zal Cleminson:

> The first rehearsal, playing 'Midnight Moses', was the catalyst. Everyone looked pleased, especially Alex. I'll admit that it took me a while to see the real potential because Alex had abandoned the James Brown voice he used with the Soul Band and had decided to sing in a less conventional manner, which I wasn't convinced about. However, it worked out okay.

Pleased with what they heard that afternoon, the two camps agreed to join forces, although it took some time for the younger half of the partnership to get used to the self-discipline and professionalism that Harvey had become accustomed to during his *Hair* days. Additionally, they were billed as Alex Harvey and Tear Gas initially, which often drew the ire of Tear Gas fans who didn't take to the lack of Tear Gas songs or the theatrical shenanigans of the old guy occupying centre stage. A young James Hamilton, who shared Harvey's love of comic books and would go on to co-found the *Forbidden Planet* chain of pop culture shops, remembers a gig at Clouds, a small venue above Green's Playhouse, on 29 June 1972. The nascent Sensational Alex Harvey Band were supporting Stone the Crows, who were trying to continue in the aftermath of losing Les Harvey. 'The abuse Alex took from the crowd that night was shocking. This is just a month or so after Les Harvey's death and they were shouting unforgivable things like 'It was the wrong Harvey brother that died''. Harvey responded by hurling abuse at the audience, and his new bandmates, their collective hearts sinking, assumed the jig was up. What they didn't realise was that not only did their new frontman thrive on confrontation, but he would also build it into the act, most memorably when Chris and Zal flanked him during 'Midnight Moses' and the trio would menacingly stare the audience out. Cleminson: 'Alex had a vision of a cohort with him as the spearhead. Everything was aimed outwards, towards imposing a 'love it or hate it' choice on the audience. It was deliberately aggressive and uncompromising'.

Bill Fehilly was bankrolling the operation, but it was Derek Nicol, an acquaintance of Fehilly's and fellow music promoter, who was in charge of the day-to-day running of the band. Together they set up Mountain Management to look after the Harvey Band and their other signing, Nazareth. It was also Nicol that came up with the Sensational Alex Harvey Band name, which was based on how Motown used to market their acts by sticking some hyperbole in front of the performers' name, for example, the Fabulous Four Tops. Harvey loved it, seeing the adjective as a challenge the band would have to live up to night in, night out, but Zal was less sure.' I never really liked the name. It sounded too much like a Showband. I preferred Tear Gas, but Alex was in charge, so the name stuck'.

The iconic logo was designed by artist Dave Field, who would also design Nazareth's most recognisable logo and produce album covers for both Mountain Management acts plus Uriah Heep, Status Quo and many others.

Soon the newly christened SAHB were in London's Morgan Studio working on their debut album *Framed*, which contained some choice covers that had long been a part of Harvey's repertoire, a couple of reworkings of earlier Harvey originals, and some new material. What is noticeable is the complete lack of co-writes with his new bandmates, or indeed any material from them at all. 'Alex already had all the songs written or chosen for the *Framed* album', explained Cleminson. 'It was a relief, I guess, to just concentrate on playing guitar'. The collaborations would come later, but for now, though, the objective was to get an album on the market as soon as possible using whatever material was at hand.

Framed was released in December 1972 and although it didn't enjoy chart success or much critical support, it did introduce one of the most distinctive voices of the 1970s, as Harvey elected, as Zal Cleminson put it above, to 'sing in a less conventional manner'. The frontman explained his reasoning in an interview with *Melody Maker*'s Harry Docherty three years after *Framed* was released: 'I went through a long period of trying to sound like Ray Charles. People said it was great. It was soul singing, but it wasn't really soul singing. It was *his* soul singing'.

'Framed' (Jerry Leiber, Mike Stoller)

Harvey had previously given this song an outing on his 1964 *Alex Harvey and His Soul Band* album, and clearly thought it strong enough to serve as both the title and opening track of his new venture with the Sensational Alex Harvey Band.

The slowed-down tempo of that earlier version is slowed even further, and Harvey has ditched the mid-Atlantic soul voice in favour of his idiosyncratic, occasionally tortured, and soon-to-be-trademark Glaswegian one, while Cleminson's guitar gives this talking blues some hard rock crunch.

'Hammer Song' (Harvey)

This is another recycled song, having previously appeared on 1969's *Roman Wall Blues*. This version begins as a guitar duet, Zal on electric and Alex on acoustic. Cleminson drops out as Harvey sings the first verse but returns for verse two, with the other band members coming in on the third. Fans of Tear Gas might frown upon this slow, gentle build-up but can breathe easy when, just after the 3.30 mark, the band explode, producing a closing two minutes heavier than anything they produced on their eponymous second album.

Nick Cave was a fan and would play several SAHB covers in his early bands, but he was clearly enamoured with 'Hammer Song', covering it on the Bad Seeds' 1986 album *Kicking Against the Pricks* (1986), and borrowing the title for one of his own compositions on *The Good Son* (1990).

'Midnight Moses' (Harvey)

'Midnight Moses' is another *Roman Wall Blues* track revisited, and whereas Harvey was already experimenting with his vocal delivery on that earlier version his new and very singular approach is now fully formed: who knew that Switzerland's second-most populated city was pronounced Juh-neev-AAAAH? Equally fully formed is the band, who are truly sensational. Zal is the star on this track, underlying Alex's vocals with clever little guitar frills throughout, and whenever Harvey takes a break, Cleminson doesn't so much play one solo as start several. It is utterly thrilling to hear as the listener has no idea in which direction he is headed. Not to be outdone, Hugh McKenna not only shores up the rhythm section but also uses a light honky-tonk piano to colour any spaces left by Cleminson, and Ted McKenna embellishes the heavy riffing with intelligent percussion. Chris Glen's bass, meanwhile, is the massive, pulsing heartbeat of the song.

The brilliant, brassy original was always going to be hard to top, but the former Tear Gas boys make it their own by making the riff as gargantuan as those on 'Smoke on the Water' or 'Paranoid'. According to Chris Glen, Harvey believed that the riff was the most important component of the song, and the feet on the monitor routine was not only about being confrontational but was also Alex's way of visually emphasising the riff.

'Midnight Moses' is the moment the Sensational Alex Harvey Band truly come alive, and it remains one of their very best songs.

'Isobel Goudie' (Harvey)

This song is regularly described as being about a prostitute, and the repeated line 'She is my lady of the night' certainly lends credence to the notion. However, Isobel *Gowdie* was a historical person, a woman of undisclosed age from Auldearn near Nairn, who was accused of witchcraft in 1662. She is infamous for her four highly detailed confessions regarding her activities as a witch, apparently given under no duress. These included having sex with the Devil, who is surely who Harvey is referring to with the phrase, 'a scaly member with a cold emission'. Although her account of her career in sorcery is comprehensive and a matter of historical record, her fate is unknown, but it is safe to assume that she was put to death by strangling and burning, the customary method of executing those guilty of witchcraft in Scotland.

The music also suggests a witch rather than a prostitute, as with its church-like organ and weird folk ambience, it could pass as the soundtrack to then-contemporary television programmes such as the *Ghost Story for Christmas* series or Nigel Kneale's one-off chiller *The Stone Tapes*. Harvey's childlike intonations in the opening lyrics only add to the overall sense of unease.

The warped folksiness is dispersed by the occasional heavy metal assault, such as at the previously mentioned 'lady of the night' lines and the *rat-a-tat-tat* delivery of the song's second part, 'Coitus Interruptus', but it soon pervades the song again like a creeping mist. It all ends with an unduly hasty fade approaching the seven-minute-thirty mark, this presumably to ensure the track fitted the vinyl release, but even at this epic length, 'Isobel Goudie' never overstays her welcome.

'Buff's Bar Blues' (Harvey)

This is a pub rock boogie that is every bit as boozy as the title suggests, and while there is no faulting the musicianship, there is a sense that, as well as recycling older material, Harvey is leaning too heavily on his bluesy past.

'I Just Want to Make Love to You' (Willie Dixon)

Harvey first gave this an outing back on 1964's *Alex Harvey and His Soul Band* album, so this is arguably another example of water-treading. However, SAHB drag it into the '70s by giving it a slow, sleazy funk makeover *à la* Sly and the Family Stone, a notion only heightened when 'Big Bud's' brass section, led by Harvey's old *Hair* mucker Bud Parkes, lurch into thrilling action towards the end.

'Hole in Her Stocking' (Harvey)

Featuring a bar room boogie piano, squealing saxes, and a bass line so 1950s it could be bequiffed, but with enough glammy reverb-drenched handclaps to reassure the listener that this is the Seventies, this is a reworking of the song Harvey originally submitted to the eponymous Rock Workshop release in 1970. This is a perfectly fine rendition, albeit one that descends into repetition and overstays its welcome, but it is that rare breed, a SAHB version, that never quite matches the raucousness of the original.

'There's No Lights on the Christmas Tree, Mother, They're Burning Big Louie Tonight' (Jim Condron, A. Harvey)

When the original version of this song, co-written with Giant Moth bandmate Condron, appeared on the Hairband's 1969 album *Band on the Wagon*, it was simply called 'Big Louie', but now it gets expanded and becomes, effectively, a complete noir short story in a single song title that reflects Harvey's love of old gangster films such as *White Heat, Little Ceasar*, and *Angels With Dirty Faces*.

Appropriately, the music evokes a vaudevillian singalong from the interwar years, which must have further distanced Tear Gas fans and left even members of the band bemused. As Cleminson memorably put it in *SAHB Story*, 'Songs like 'Hole in Her Stocking' and 'Big Louie' didn't always convince you that the path would be paved with sweat-encrusted maidens wallowing at your feet'.

'Big Louie' was SAHB's first-ever single, released in December 1972. Like Jona Lewie's 'Stop the Cavalry', its claim to be a Christmas song is tenuous; unlike 'Stop the Cavalry', 'Big Louie' has appeared on precisely no *Best Christmas Album in the World... Ever*.

'St. Anthony' (Harvey)

The story of Saint Anthony the Great enduring supernatural temptation in the Egyptian desert has been the subject of artists from the tenth century on, and according to Harvey biographer John Neil Munro, the singer was 'loosely' inspired by Hieronymus Bosch's depiction of the event. Anthony being offered sex by a demon in the form of a beautiful woman is a standard scenario in the temptation legend, and it is this aspect that Harvey focuses on lyrically, telling us that 'She comes around when the sun goes down/Saying c'mon, baby, you can risk it', whereupon she ties the holy man to his bed and gives him a right good seeing-to of Biblical proportions.

Musically, this is blues-soaked heavy metal reminiscent of Led Zeppelin and is Cleminson's *Framed* favourite.

Related Songs
'The Harp' (Holub, I. Milner, J. Milner, Harvey)
This, the non-album B-side to 'Big Louie', is an English translation by Ian
and Jarmilla Milner of a poem by Czech writer Miroslav Holub (1923-1998)
with music by Harvey. Its distinct Middle Eastern flavour makes it sound
like a holdover from the psychedelic Sixties, but by adapting a non-English
language poem to music, Harvey was blazing the trail later followed by fellow
Scots troubadour Jackie Leven.

Next – The Sensational Alex Harvey Band

Personnel:
Alex Harvey: vocals, harmonica, guitar
Zal Cleminson: guitar, vocals
Hugh McKenna: electric piano, piano, organ, vocals
Chris Glen: bass guitar, vocals
Ted McKenna: drums, percussion, vocals
David Batchelor: backing vocals
Pip Williams: arrangements on 'Swampsnake', Gang Bang', 'Next', and 'The Last of the Teenage Idols'
Produced at Audio International Studios, London, and Apple Studios, London, by Phil Wainman and the Sensational Alex Harvey Band
Release Date: November 1973
Label: Vertigo
Highest Chart Place: UK 37
Running time: 35:54

Establishing the band had been the mission statement of 1972, but now it was time to work on the band's visual identity. Harvey had already adopted the long-sleeved, black and white hooped t-shirt as his stage attire, but none of the other familiar elements were in place, including arguably the most instantly recognisable visual component of SAHB, Cleminson's clown face. The guitarist discussed the thinking behind the mime make-up with online magazine *The College Crowd Digs Me*:

> Well, when I started playing, I looked at other guitar players playing their solos. The angst, the whole posing with facial expressions. And I just thought it was hilarious (laughs). So, I took it upon myself to sort of stage what they were doing in a kind of comic way. And it got a reaction from the fans.
> But then, as the band got bigger and we started to play bigger and bigger venues, our manager says, 'Look, the people at the back of the hall cannot see what you're doing. They cannot see all those expressions. They can't see all of that stuff.' So, we looked at ways I could project it in bigger venues.

One early idea was to cover Zal's face in green Letraset dots, which would certainly have been memorable but not necessarily for the right reasons. Thankfully, this concept never got off the drawing board and seeing a performance by the famous French mime artist Marcel Marceau pointed Cleminson in the right direction. Mime, he realised, was the perfect medium 'to exploit my ironic guitar hero persona'.

In terms of clothing, Harvey wanted SAHB to avoid one specific look, such as the double-denim of Status Quo or the Bay City Rollers' tartan, and have each member of the band adopt their own distinctive style. Between Hugh's shapeless smoking jacket/dressing gown affair and Ted's suits and shorts combo, it is safe to say the McKenna cousins got the sartorial short shrift, but the three front-of-stage players fared better. Harvey had his hoops, of course, which he augmented with his Captain Hook pirate coat, or a leather jacket, or a trench coat, depending on the song being performed. Chris Glen became the band's Pretty Boy Blue, with his open chest jerkin, neckerchief, and exterior codpiece, while Cleminson sported distinctive green, yellow and black jumpsuits as well as the white face, essentially inventing the Kiss look before Kiss did.

The costumes were made by Bambi Ballard, who had worked in film, theatre, and fashion before deciding to specialise in fashion for rock and pop stars. Apart from the Harvey Band, her clients included Elkie Brooks, The Sweet, Procol Harum, and Steeleye Span. Ironically, Ballard was also behind the uniform Bay City Rollers look that Harvey wanted to avoid.

Suitably attired, SAHB sallied forth on a five-date tour supporting Mott the Hoople in late February/early March, and then were out on the road again from the end of May supporting Slade. Although Cleminson remembers both Mott and Slade making them feel very welcome, the Slade fans were somewhat less accommodating. Chris Charlesworth of *Melody Maker* reported that SAHB received 'a rough reception – rather like the Christians fighting lions in front of a patriotic Roman audience', while in the *NME,* Nick Kent opined that 'The Sensational Alex Harvey Band were barely stomached by the crowd'. Cleminson concurs: 'SAHB had a do-or-die attitude when playing support. We saw it as an opportunity to impress. Some Slade fans found us a bit arrogant and confusing, so they gave us a hard time. Alex promptly went off stage, found a water pistol to piss in and sprayed them while grinning that inimitable grin ...'

The next memorable date in the diary was 21 July, the Buxton Pop Festival, an event best remembered for the audience and some of the performers being terrorised by Hell's Angels, whom Alex took to task from the stage. Chris Glen remembers Buxton as the gig SAHB arrived, not just because of Harvey's ability to influence the crowd but also how tightly the band functioned as a unit: 'Alex didn't say anything to us, he just waved his arm, and we stopped dead like it had been rehearsed'. It also marked the first time one of the rock fraternity, in this case of Pete Agnew of Mountain labelmates, Nazareth, told him they would not like to have to follow SAHB on stage. It wouldn't be the last.

The London Music Festival followed on 5 August, with SAHB supporting Manfred Mann's Earth Band and headliners Uriah Heep. As with the Slade tour, SAHB were poorly received, as long delays between the acts led to a crowd already restless for Heep to turn apoplectic when Harvey opened with a version of the Osmonds' 'Crazy Horses'. The inevitable shower of not-always-empty plastic beer containers rained down on the band. Fan Steve Toal, interviewed in Munro's *The Sensational Alex Harvey,* believed the singer was deliberately trying to goad the Heep audience, aware that a poor reaction would garner just as many column inches as a positive one. Given Harvey's confrontational nature, this sounds entirely plausible, but it is equally possible Alex just loved the song, being an environmentalist long before such concerns became a *cause célèbre* amongst the rock fraternity. The fact the band recorded the Osmonds hit for *The Penthouse Tapes* three years later certainly suggests Harvey didn't view the song solely as a crowd-baiter.

An altogether more positive response awaited the band at the Reading Festival on 25 August when they unveiled a new song, 'The Faith Healer', just as the sun was going down, and is discussed below. SAHB's final support slot for the year was a short European jaunt in the company of those doyens of double denim, Status Quo, which included a stop at Harvey's early Sixties stomping ground, Hamburg. This was almost immediately followed by the band's first headlining tour, a 32-day trek around the UK with hard-rocking proggers Beckett in tow, who would release their sole album the following year. The tour, which took in such C-list venues as Ayr Pavilion, Newcastle Polytechnic, and the Greyhound in Croydon, was in support of the band's second album, *Next*, which had been released in November.

Recruited to give the album a commercial spit and polish was Phil Wainman, a choice that underwhelmed Zal Cleminson. Here he is talking to the online magazine *It's Psychedelic Baby*:

> It was produced by Phil Wainman, who produced Sweet. I could say 'enough said'. However, with hindsight, it was clear that our record company wanted to see the band on *Top of the Pops*. But for me, the competition wasn't Sweet or Mud or, heaven forbid, Gary Glitter. For me, the competition was Led Zeppelin, Deep Purple and Pink Floyd. I honestly believe SAHB never really recovered from that mindset.

Next didn't chart upon initial release but eventually reached number 37 on 23 August 1975 on the back of the chart success of *The Impossible Dream* and *Tomorrow Belongs To Me*, and through the band continuing to build its audience via incessant touring.

The band closed the year with their first television appearance on the prestigious *Old Grey Whistle Test*. This was the BBC's late-night music show that included live sessions, concert footage, and interviews, and was a proven career maker. SAHB performed 'Faith Healer' and 'Next', the latter of which is discussed below.

'Swampsnake' (Harvey, H. McKenna)
As well as being the album opener, 'Swampsnake' was the first song written by the writing team of Alex Harvey and Hugh McKenna, and it is their first instant classic. The initial driver of 'Swampsnake' is McKenna's piano, but it is soon buried beneath a giddy mix of Harvey's staccato harmonica, Cleminson's pseudo-slide guitar and Ted McKenna's off-beat and off-the-beat percussion.

The arrangement is so dense it runs the risk of becoming as muddy as the Mississippi, but Phil Wainman's pop chops keep things crisp and lively. Lyrics such as 'Let me wash the windows/Let me clean away your sin' add a touch of bayou gothic, and the result is a bluesy pop romp with emphasis on the pop.

'Gang Bang' (Harvey, H. McKenna)
'There were twenty-seven guys' and 'She just kept on rockin' 'til the night was gone' soon dispels any hope that the title 'Gang Bang' is a metaphor or euphemism. The '70s, eh? In the sleeve notes of early SAHB compilation *Big Hits and Close Shaves*, Harvey himself dismissed the lyrics as 'rubbish', stating 'There's no glory in rape'.

Musically, this stalks the same territory as 'Swampsnake' but with an uncredited horn section, possibly Big Bud's Brass from the previous album, and a leaning to what Bob Seger would soon term 'Old Time Rock and Roll'. If you can get past the misogyny of the words this is a fun track, although one very much in the shadow of its predecessor.

'The Faith Healer' (Harvey, H. McKenna)
That rhythmic 'doo-doo-doo-doo-doo-doo' that opens 'The Faith Healer' is created using a Tootalbug Drone, a device devised by Hairband saxophonist and flautist Ashton Tootal. It had several settings, but according to Cleminson, they all went 'doo-doo-doo-doo-doo-doo'. Joining the drone in the extended instrumental opening are maracas and other percussion effects, an assortment of whistles, and Cleminson's distinctive four-chord riff, before Harvey starts singing at the two-minute thirty mark. According to Glen, this introduction was born less by creativity and more by pragmatism, producer Wainman stretching it to ensure that both sides of the cassette tape were of equal length.

'The Faith Healer' is the first SAHB song that Harvey inhabits rather than just sings, and the song has a more pronounced, and menacing, American gothic feel than 'Swampsnake'. Harvey may be offering 'everlasting sweet desire' but does so while channelling Robert Mitchum's *Night of the Hunter* character Harry Powell. 'Let me put my hands on you?' No thanks.

What with the hypnotic intro and Harvey's charismatic vocal performance, it is no wonder 'The Faith Healer' was such a show stealer at the 1973 Reading Festival. Interviewed for *SAHB Stories*, Hugh McKenna recalled:

> The moment Alex put his hands up in the twin V-sign pose and sang, 'Let me put my hands on you', I just knew it was going to be magic. I had a premonition, the one and only one I've had in my life. As soon as we came off, I told the guys, wait till you see the press next week, it's going to be all about us. I was absolutely certain we were going to cop all the press. Rod Stewart was on, Status Quo were on – big, big names, but we absolutely slew everybody.

Ted McKenna felt the same: 'That was the point when I think we all felt that this was all really happening, and we really had something'.

Talking to *The College Crowd Digs Me* website, Cleminson identified the Temptations' 1970 single 'Ball Of Confusion' as surprising inspiration behind 'Faith Healer', and there are undeniable structural similarities, not least the Tootalbug Drone homaging the repetitive brass motive employed by the Funk Brothers throughout the Temptations' song.

Alas, the Tootalbug never caught on outside the SAHB camp and, apart from a couple of *Hair* soundtrack albums, its inventor appeared on only one other recording, a 1977 National Youth Jazz Orchestra album produced in conjunction with the Campaign for Real Ale and featuring such ditties as 'Ruddle's Rutland Reflections' and 'Samuel Smith and His Amazing Dancing Bear'. I'll wait while you head over to *Discogs* to check its availability.

'Giddy Up a Ding Dong' (Freddie Bell, Joey Lattanzi)

'Giddy Up a Ding Dong' was originally recorded by Freddie Bell and the Bellboys and popularised via their appearance in the 1956 film *Rock Around the Clock*. It reached number four in the UK singles chart. According to various sources, including the *Scotsman* newspaper, the Bellboys were the first American rock and roll group to play Glasgow, and assuming Harvey was in the audience is hardly a stretch. The following year it was covered by none other than 'England's Alex Harvey', Tommy Steele.

The Harvey Band version doesn't deviate from the original, although Wainman glams it up a little by introducing Chinn-Chapman-approved handclaps. It was released as a single, backed by 'Buff's Bar Blues' from *Framed*, in October 1973 to little fanfare and even less success. Even the band weren't fans. Here is Chris Glen, from his autobiography *The Bass Business*:

> *Next* went well, but we still didn't have a hit single, which is what we had been asked for. Phil's idea of a hit single had a particular Sweet, Mud kind of beat to it, and the nearest we had was 'Giddy Up A Ding Dong'. So that was the single, and not 'Faith Healer', which would have been much better for us. It still gets played... who plays 'Giddy Up A Ding Dong'?

In *SAHB Stories*, Cleminson is more succinct: 'Giddy Up A Ding Dong? Shite!'

That said, a video of the band performing it on a European pop show can be found on YouTube. It features a priceless example of the fun choreography that was becoming a feature of SAHB's live shows, and both Cleminson and Glen, consummate professionals, give it their all. Cleminson explained the origins of the dance routines in the SAHB set:

> We all had a penchant for a dance routine – in Scotland, one is taught the art of Scottish Country Dancing at an early age. We also admired many of the black soul bands who also moved beautifully. We incorporated a whole

range of memorable routines to suit the music. The effect was very tongue-in-cheek – vaudevillian.

'Next' (Jacques Brel, Mort Shuman, Eric Blau)

The French military made use of mobile brothels (Bordels Mobiles de Campagne, or BMCs) during both world wars and the First Indochina War to supply prostitution to French soldiers, with the last BMC, serving the Foreign Legion in Djibouti, closing as late as 2003.

Jacques Brel's 1964 song 'Au Suivant', translated by Shuman and Blau as 'Next', tells of a young soldier traumatised by the impersonal, almost industrial way he loses his virginity by being processed through a BMC: 'I was just a child, a hundred like me/I followed a naked body, a naked body followed me'. Even in later life, the soldier is haunted by his experience, unable to enjoy sex without hearing the sergeant's voice, 'a voice that stinks of whisky/Of corpses and of mud', commanding 'Next! Next!'

The song had previously been covered by Scott Walker, possibly the most prolific English language interpreter of Brel's work, but his reading is hampered by a distracting Disney-esque 'April showers' arrangement and he approaches the song like a singer, admittedly an immensely voiced one, whereas Harvey opts to perform it as an actor. The *NME*'s Charles Shaar Murray best describes Harvey's superior handling of 'Next':

Alex Harvey had the insight to locate the central core of the song and the passion to get him to that core. His performance of Jacques Brel's 'Next' is purest bravura, and it works precisely because Harvey reduced the distance between himself and the song to nothing. He became the song, was utterly present in the song and, by doing so, pulled the listener right in there himself.

The string quartet is arranged by Pip Williams, who also provided arrangements for 'Swampsnake', 'Gang Bang', 'and 'Last of the Teenage Idols'. At this point in his career, Williams was best known as a session guitarist, having played on all the early Sweet hits, but would later move into production; he was in the sound booth for many a Status Quo album, beginning with *Rocking All Over the World* (1977). As he recalls in the documentary *Total Rock Review: The Sensational Alex Harvey Band*, he got a call from producer Phil Wainman, who said, 'I'm working with this character Alex Harvey. Blimey, I don't know what I've bitten off here, but it may be more than I can chew', and asked Williams to do the scores. Williams got a brief from Harvey that the score for 'Next' be somewhat Parisian sounding, a mood already suggested in the Brel original, and that it be 'both saccharine and sinister'. The singer also suggested the tango arrangement.

SAHB appeared on the BBC's *The Old Grey Whistle Test* on 20 December, one of those moments that would have everyone talking in the schoolyard the next day were it not the Christmas holidays. For their performance of 'Next' they were accompanied by a bizarrely masked string quartet hired from the Johnny Dankworth Orchestra. For the few seconds that you see him, it is clear Cleminson fancies his chances at upstaging Harvey, but he and Ted McKenna receive scant lens time, and Glen and Hugh McKenna are all but rendered invisible, the camera totally mesmerised, held spellbound by Harvey's compelling performance as he conveys the pain and anger and bitterness of Brel's soldier through facial expression alone. Entirely bereft of props or effects, it is a stunning piece of rock theatre.

'Vambo Marble Eye' (Harvey, H. McKenna, Cleminson, Glen, T. McKenna)
The first complete band-written song also marks the debut of Harvey's superheroic alter-ego Vambo. In terms of some of the lyrical content and vocal delivery, 'Vambo Marble Eye' is essentially a dress rehearsal for 'The Hot City Symphony Part 1: Vambo' from the band's third album, *The Impossible Dream*. Musically, it is not Vambo that rules but wah-wah pedals – Cleminson hails this as his personal favourite from *Next* precisely because of the wah-wah solo – resulting in a funkathon that nods to the likes of Isaac Hayes and Sly Stone.

'The Last of the Teenage Idols' (Harvey, H. McKenna, Cleminson)
The album finale takes the form of a structure very much in vogue with prog rockers of the time, the song suite, without taking on board any of prog's baroque frilliness. Cleminson: "Teenage Idol' was born from a riff I had since Tear Gas. Alex and Hugh were the most prolific songwriters. It was a fruitful collaboration. For my part, I offered whatever guitar part suited the song, including many improvised solos'.

The song starts as a piano ballad, Harvey inviting the listener to address him by several nonsensical identities, such as the Sheikh of Tomorrow, while Hugh McKenna provides plaintive support. This section would be happy at home on any then-current Billy Joel or Randy Newman album. The rest of the band join in for verse two, keeping the same melody but giving it a hard rocking edge.

The second part of the song suite continues to rock out but takes a subtle musical shift back in time to Harvey's big band soul set-up. The only thing missing is a brass section, which would have lifted this otherwise slightly aimless midsection. No matter, for it doesn't overstay its welcome, as part three, travelling even further back, abruptly becomes a doo-wop tune, played straight and aching with Fifties teen heartbreak, as Harvey, in a nod to his brief life as Scotland's Tommy Steele, reminisces how he 'was the winner of the Teenage Idol competition'.

'Last of the Teenage Idols' provides a strong finish to a strong album and would lend its title to the ultimate Harvey retrospective, a 217-track, 14-disc anthology released in 2016 covering all stages of the singer's career.

Above: 'Good evening, boys and girls. I'd like to introduce you to my band, the Sensational Alex Harvey Band'. L-R: Chris Glen, Ted McKenna, Alex Harvey, Hugh McKenna, Zal Cleminson.

Right: The 'cohort' saw Harvey flanked by Glen and Cleminson – it was a feature of every performance.

Left: The design of Harvey's debut album is classy and minimalistic, but don't believe everything you read on the cover. (*Universal*)

Right: Alex's first solo album *The Blues* is almost precisely that. The only other player is his brother Leslie. (*Universal*)

Left: Alex was inspired to write the title track of *Roman Wall Blues* after being given a book of W. H. Auden's poetry as a gift. (*Universal*)

Right: Tear Gas's debut had some solid sounds, a striking cover and an intriguing title, but little in the way of sales. (*Esoteric/Cherry Red Records*)

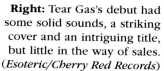

Left: I could never quite make it out, but thanks to Chris Glen's autobiography, I now know that the cover of Tear Gas's self-titled second depicts someone crushing an egg. (*Esoteric/ Cherry Red Records*)

Right: *Caveat emptor*: Following the success of SAHB, the 1972 oddball *The Joker Is Wild* was re-released as *This Is The Sensational Alex Harvey Band* – it wasn't. (*Metronome*)

Left: *Framed*'s underwhelming die-cut cover. Fortunately, the album itself was something special. (*Mercury/Universal*)

Right: Producer Phil Wainman was part of the team behind The Sweet's chart success, and he brings polish to SAHB's firepower on *Next*. (*Mercury/Universal*)

Left: Harvey's rock 'n' roll dreams and comic book fantasies come true when *The Impossible Dream* becomes his first charting album. (*Mercury/Universal*)

Right: The logo of *Tomorrow Belongs To Me* is inspired by that of the long-running science fiction magazine *Amazing Stories*. (*Mercury/Universal*)

Left: Tear Gas frontman David Batchelor moved into production and *Live!* is his masterpiece. The best live album ever? It has got to be a contender. (*Universal*)

Right: The B in SAHB finally makes the front cover with *The Penthouse Tapes*, but this ragtag collection of covers and leftovers is their weakest set. (*Mercury/Universal*)

Left: Alex on *The Old Grey Whistle Test* (*OGWT*). Harvey was a master at working the camera; that laser-eyed stare could leave viewers feeling uncomfortable. (*BBC*)

Right: Cleminson's mime makeup evolved over time. Here, he is sporting an early version on *OGWT* performing 'The Faith Healer'. (*BBC*)

Left: Harvey on *OGWT* performing 'Next'. He doesn't so much sing the song as inhabit it. (*BBC*)

Right: SAHB celebrate the American Bicentennial performing 'Boston Tea Party' on *Top Of The Pops*. (*BBC*)

Left: A grizzled Harvey, just back from hunting the Loch Ness Monster, makes a return trip to the *TOTP* studios to promote 'Boston Tea Party'. (*BBC*)

Right: Chris and Zal come over all vaudevillian performing 'Delilah' on *OGWT*, May 1975. (*BBC*)

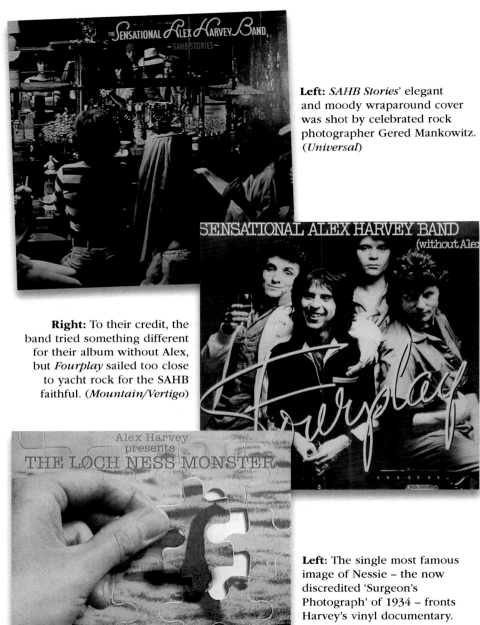

Left: *SAHB Stories'* elegant and moody wraparound cover was shot by celebrated rock photographer Gered Mankowitz. (*Universal*)

Right: To their credit, the band tried something different for their album without Alex, but *Fourplay* sailed too close to yacht rock for the SAHB faithful. (*Mountain/Vertigo*)

Left: The single most famous image of Nessie – the now discredited 'Surgeon's Photograph' of 1934 – fronts Harvey's vinyl documentary. (*K-Tel/Voiceprint*)

Right: Jacob Einstein's 1916 sculpture *Torso In Metal from The Rock Drill* is the cover star of SAHB's swan song. The original is on display at the Tate Modern. (*Mercury/Universal*)

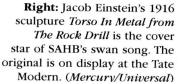

Left: Harvey's first post-SAHB release, 1979's *The Mafia Stole My Guitar* was also the last album he would release in his lifetime. (*RCA/Sony*)

Right: Harvey's reworking of 'Roman Wall Blues' on this posthumous release would have fitted alongside then-contemporary acts like Big Country and U2, but the rest was a harder sell in 1982. (*Powerstation/Edsel*)

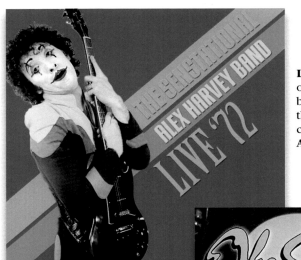

Left: This oddity appears only on Spotify. Despite being namechecked twice on the cover, is it possible the compilers didn't know what Alex Harvey looked like?

Right: This excellent set collects all of SAHB's recordings for the BBC, including two tracks from the SAHB (Without Alex) album *Fourplay*. (*Universal/BBC Music*)

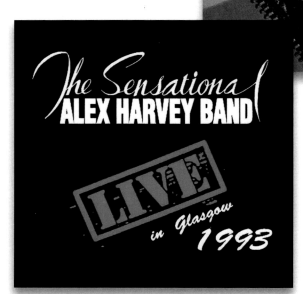

Left: SAHB briefly reunited in the 1990s, but the designer of this album sleeve clearly didn't understand the visual aspect of the band. (*Meantime Records*)

Right: This 14-CD retrospective came in a handsome slipcase designed by SAHB's 21st-century frontman Max Maxwell. (*Universal*)

Left: *Shout* is an excellent and inexpensive introduction to Alex Harvey, but interested parties should move fast, as at this time of writing, it appears to be going out of print. (*Spectrum/Universal Music*)

Right: A 1950s photo of Alex fronts this intriguing collection of oddities from the 1960s. (*Alchemy Entertainment*)

Left: Harvey liked his comic books. Here's a press ad for the 'Runaway' single depicting Alex as a Dennis the Menace-type character. (*Author's collection*)

Right: This press ad for the 'Sergeant Fury' single features Harvey's favourite Marvel hero as depicted by John Severin on the cover of *Sgt. Fury And His Howling Commandos* 74. (*Author's collection*)

Left: And finally, the art on the cover of the 'Jungle Jenny' single 'apes' Frank Thorne's *Moonshine McJugs* comic strip for *Playboy*. (*Universal/Vertigo*)

Right: More comic book shenanigans. Everyone, bar Ted McKenna, on the cover of the 1976 UK Tour programme was plagiarised from *Spider-Man* illustrations by Marvel artist John Romita. (*Author's collection*)

Left: The first Knebworth Festival, the scene of SAHB's legendary – and perhaps mythical – confrontation with The Doobie Brothers.

Left: Glasgow remembers Alex 1: 'A shrunken head of my father', is what Alex Harvey Jr. called this smaller-than-life-size bust at its unveiling. But that was okay because 'he used to collect things like that'. (*Peter Gallagher*)

Below: Glasgow remembers Alex 2: Like the bust, this bench once resided in the city's now-closed Winter Gardens. Its current whereabouts are uncertain. (*Peter Gallagher*)

The Sensational
Alex Harvey
5th February 1935 ~ 4th February 1982
Vambo Still Rool

Right: Glasgow remembers Alex 3: A tree grows in Vibrania (AKA Glasgow Green). (*Peter Gallagher*)

The Sensational Alex Harvey
5th Feb 1935 - 4th Feb 19 ˙
Vambo he go on him w e/
He come back some sunny day
He go home now
Hail Vibrania!

Left: Glasgow remembers Alex 4: The author in front of Alex's portrait in the Clutha mural. It has now been painted over. (*Owen Gallagher*)

Left: Alice Cooper, Noddy Holder and Stan Lee are amongst those joining SAHB in wishing Alex a happy 40th. Who else can you spot? (*Author's collection*)

Right: The 21st-century SAHB as depicted by new frontman Max Maxwell.

The Impossible Dream – The Sensational Alex Harvey Band

Personnel:
Alex Harvey: vocals, rhythm guitar
Zal Cleminson: guitar
Hugh McKenna: keyboards, synthesiser
Chris Glen: bass guitar
Ted McKenna: drums
Vicky Silva: Vocals on 'Anthem'
London-Scottish TA Regiment: drums and pipes on 'Anthem'
Produced at Apple Studios, London, by David Batchelor and the Sensational Alex Harvey Band. 'Sergeant Fury' produced by Derek Wadsworth
Release Date: October 1974
Label: Vertigo
Highest Chart Place: UK 16
Running time: 43:09

'The year 1974 has really seen the emergence of the band as one of the most popular and exciting rock acts in Britain'. So wrote the unidentified scribe of the mighty *Coleshill Chronicle*'s 'Musicbox' column, and his or her mother didn't raise no Dixie-whistler.

That said, there was a bit of a wobble early in the year when it came to recording the third album, then titled *Can't Get Enough*. Phil Wainman was unavailable, so the call went out to Shel Talmy, a Brit-based American who had produced a classic run of hit singles for The Kinks and The Who in the 1960s. With such a pedigree, Talmy seemed the ideal choice for the SAHBs, but the band were less than chuffed with the results. 'There we were again, trying to bring in someone that could create hip music', said Cleminson in *SAHB Stories*, but 'It was all dull and muffled – there was no energy or life in it'. At a playback of the record, the band members expressed their disappointment to manager Bill Fehilly, who agreed to foot the bill for re-recording the whole album. The Talmy sessions would see the light of day in 2009 as *Hot City: The 1974 Unreleased Album*, which will be discussed in a later chapter.

The band returned to the studio for a second stab at the album in July, this time with former Tear Gas singer David Batchelor on board as producer. Alex explained the choice to *Melody Maker*'s Harry Docherty:

Because Davey Batchelor drove the band about. He was doin' our sound. We were all sittin' in the same car goin' tae gigs, and stayin' in the same hotel, and that's why. He was there while songs were being constructed, sittin' in a car, that's when most of the rehearsal is done really. Davey was always well intae sound gear, so we thought we'd give it a go, keep it in the family. Since then, we've carried on doin' it. He always was a member of the band.

The omnipresent and ever-necessary road ran right through the centre of the two recording sessions, with a twenty-three-date UK tour kicking off on 9 May and concluding exactly a month later. Support came from Strider, a two-album hard rock band that would be defunct before the year was out. The fifth date of the tour, at the Swansea Top Rank Suite, was a poignant and painful one for Alex, this being the site of Les Harvey's death two years earlier.

4 June found the band at the Rainbow Theatre, London, where their four-song set – 'Vambo', 'Sergeant Fury', 'Framed', and Sly and the Family Stone's 'Dance to the Music' – was filmed for the American ABC television show *In Concert*. Also appearing that night, and for the same purpose, were Procol Harum, Foghat, and, incongruously, Jim Stafford, who, it will be remembered, didn't like spiders and snakes. The show was broadcast a month later, on 5 July.

The band played the first ever Knebworth Festival, then dubbed the 'Bucolic Frolic', on 20 July. The only British outfit on the bill, they were slotted between the increasingly *avant-garde* Tim Buckley and jazz-fusionists the Mahavishnu Orchestra, but it was the home-grown talent that, according to the *Daily Mirror*'s Deborah Thomas, 'grabbed hold of the Knebworth Pop Festival like a pack of ravening wolves'.

Writing a tribute to Harvey on the thirtieth anniversary of his death, the *Scotsman*'s Anna Burnside recalled how the second-billed Doobie Brothers' minders tried to eject the Harvey Band from their backstage caravan. Harvey growled, 'You can tell the Doobie Brothers if they want this caravan, they're going to have to fight us for it. With knives'. Harvey may have been a pacifist, but he could still play the Glasgow hardman when the occasion called for it. The Doobies declined the invitation. It is a brilliant rock and roll story, and Burnside is far from the first to tell it, but Chris Glen scuppers it in *SAHB Story*:

> Then we had an argument with the Doobie Brothers. They'd got the wrong dressing room and they were in ours, so Alex and I went and gave it the Glaswegian, this is oor fuckin' dressin' room… They went, We're leaving! That's all it was, there wasn't any knife action or any of the stories people tell you.

That's considerably less brilliant than the 'knives version', so little wonder music writers take a leaf out of *The Man Who Shot Liberty Valance* playbook: 'When the legend becomes fact, print the legend'.

On 23 August, by which time they had put the finishing touches on their new album, now called *The Impossible Dream*, the band were back at the Reading Festival on a bill that included 10cc and Camel. Significantly, SAHB were now the headliners. Once he got over the lack of Status Quo (the organisers 'biggest mistake was the failure to book the well-known boogie band', apparently), Geoff Thompson of the *Bracknell Times* was won over by SAHB, more specifically Zal Cleminson. 'A fanfare introduced the band led by Alex and his sidekick Zal Cleminson on lead guitar. Boy! How this band can rock, with Zally' – Zally? – 'ripping out some fine solos. Zal, as last year, was decked out in his jester's outfit with his whitened face, but he sure can play that guitar'. The music weeklies were equally approving but lacked Thompson's nerdy enthusiasm.

Tomorrow Belongs to Me was released in October, Vertigo promoting the album with a truly dreadful slogan more designed to bamboozle record buyers rather than win converts:

It's whimsy! It's flash! It's rowdy! It's vaudeville! It's woolly! It's droll! It's perverse! It's here! It's The Sensational Alex Harvey Band's new album *The Impossible Dream*.

The cover by Keith Davis, depicting Alex as the star of his own comic book atop a stack of other 1950s-styled comics, was in keeping with how Harvey viewed the music. 'The album represents certain fantasies of mine', he said on a promotional interview disc, 'comic book fantasies, if you like'.

Long-time SAHB supporter Charles Shaar Murray was ecstatic, telling his *NME* readers that *The Impossible Dream* was 'one mo-fo of a rock and roll album', stating that the 'Hot City Symphony' two-parter 'demonstrates quite convincingly exactly what lifts the SAHB into the First Division (and make no mistake about it — they *are* a First Div. band even though not enough people have sussed it yet)'. Over in *Melody Maker*, Allan Jones, who dubbed the SAHB sound 'switchblade rock' was equally enthusiastic, calling the record 'an essential album', and urging, 'Now more than ever TURN IT UP'.

More importantly, a decent chunk of the record-buying public agreed and sent the album into the UK top twenty, where it peaked at 16.

The band had no time to rest on its laurels, however, as a new album meant a new tour, so off they went on a thirteen-date British jaunt that lasted from 3 to 19 October. In support were short-lived pub rockers Slack Alice, whose keyboard player John Cook would form Midnight Flyer with Maggie Bell in the 1980s. As with the album, the tour was a hit with fans and critics alike, with *Birmingham Daily Post*'s music pundit dubbing a SAHB show 'theatre for the working class' and observing that 'Zal Cleminson's original guitar playing and his leery clowning compliments Harvey nicely'.

Having conquered their homeland, SAHB set their sights on America. Their first US tour kicked off on 15 November, and although they served as support to the likes of Manfred Mann's Earth Band and the J. Geils Band on some dates, they also had some key headlining shows, including a five-night residency at the Whisky a Go Go from 20 – 24th November. *Billboard*'s Bob Kirsch liked what he saw on opening night:

Harvey gave the Whisky what amounted to a genuine theatrical production. Harvey's voice moves alternately and early from a whisper to a scream and various in-between stages yet it is always well controlled. The band is far more than adequate' – clearly Kirsch kept it cool when it came to praise – 'and the material all works. The 39-year-old rocker can draw sadness and laughter from an audience and is a true original who, with proper exposure, could become one of the major rock names in this country as well as in England.

Another headline show was at the celebrated 2,700-capacity Agora Theatre and Ballroom in Cleveland, Ohio, on 9 December. In attendance was future giant of rock photography Janet Macoska, then a 20-year-old student covering the gig for her college newspaper, but she wasn't only there in a professional capacity.

I was already a fan because WMMS Radio in Cleveland, who were fabulous at featuring and promoting new acts, had been playing their music. The band was also featured on a late-night music show *In Concert*, which was the first time I'd seen them live. They did three songs and blew me away. I'd never seen any band like SAHB. For shows at the Agora, you had to arrive early and claim your spot so a couple of friends and myself did that so I could be up front to do photographs. They did NOT disappoint.

College newspapers were hugely important to music and venue managers when it came to selling tickets. Macoska: 'The audience they wanted to reach specifically were the college-aged kids. That was the audience that would give new bands a chance, and they were six steps ahead of regular media like the daily press. I guess I would compare it to kids today with Tik Tok and other online media. They are locked into their media. College kids had their ears on the radio for new music'.

Macoska also conducted a telephone interview with Harvey and published her SAHB article under a bold headline: 'Alex Harvey is Rock's Next Superstar!' What was it that impressed her about the band?

Everything impressed me about Alex and the band's performance. His charisma and presence onstage were so powerful, and his supporting cast were a finely tuned menacing mob. They were edgy, intelligent, humorous, and thoroughly entertaining. *Memorable*. Keep in mind that I was 20 years old, and just starting in my career photographing rock and roll, so I hadn't seen tons of bands at that time, but as a lifelong rock and roll fan, I knew they were way above anything else I'd seen or heard. The *energy* they put out had the same grit and power as the music.

This was Janet's first SAHB experience, but as we shall see, it would not be her last. Meanwhile, the tour juggernaut rolled relentlessly on, concluding after 22 cities in New York. For a rock band from Glasgow, touring America, the birthplace of the genre, must have been like all their Christmases had come at once. Zal Cleminson:

Anything to do with touring America informed a lifelong dream for all of us, especially for Alex. He saw the USA as a spiritual homecoming, as most of his musical influences were early American rock and roll. Touring the USA gave the band a powerful sense of achievement, even in those backwater states where we were often viewed equally with extreme prejudice and bewilderment. Certain other cities and towns, like Cleveland, Pittsburgh, Dallas, LA, and New York, really took to the band's music and its overt presence.

We will touch on why the band was successful in those territories later, but the 1974 American Tour held one last surprise for Alex. New York is the home of Marvel Comics, so Harvey took a punt and invited Marvel supremo Stan Lee to the band's send-off, a lunch at the city's Plaza Hotel. Much to the singer's delight and astonishment, the man called The Man accepted. 'Can you imagine?', Alex beamed to the *NME*. 'Any man like that who would just come to my party, well, it's fantastic. Charles Shaar Murray met him in London and told him how much I idolised him; I've got so many of those comics'.

Partying with Stan the Man; sold out shows in the United States; sold out shows in Britain; headlining the Reading Festival; and an album in the UK top twenty. It had taken the better part of twenty years, but at last, a star was born. The Impossible Dream had come true.

'Hot City Symphony Part 1: Vambo' (Harvey, H. McKenna)

This song, henceforth abbreviated to 'Vambo', opens with Ted tenderising the skins with the kind of tribal zeal later favoured by Animal of The Muppets. Cleminson joins with a jarring three-note guitar pattern, the gap between each repetition decreasing in sync with the pattern's increasing shrillness. In comes Glen on bass, and the disquieting dissonance increases further until suddenly, brilliantly, it's gone, replaced by classic rock riffery that grabs the listener by the scruff of the neck and might even surpass that of the mighty 'Midnight Moses'. It is a touch of (relatively) quiet genius that demonstrates that SAHB didn't rely solely on visuals for theatricality, as is the wonderful middle eight where Hugh and Zal solo off against each other like squabbling toys.

According to Hugh McKenna, the section before the riffing was inspired by Persian marching music by a tribe called the Booids 'that Alex had seen in some BBC documentary'. Now, the BBC is well-known for its founding mantra of 'to inform, educate, and entertain', but that sounds like an extremely niche piece of programming, and sho' nuff, a quick online search for 'Booids' offers up but two options, the booidea family of snakes or a tune by... The Sensational Alex Harvey Band! Sounds like 'the Booids' was Alex telling another lion-tamer story.

Vambo is back, and although Harvey often described him as a cross between Santa Claus and Captain Marvel (or sometimes Spider-Man, Les Harvey's favourite superhero), he comes across as someone bound more by civic responsibility than abundant seasonal generosity or the foiling of ne'er-do-wells. 'Vambo', we are informed, 'never vandal be/Vambo never cut down tree'. Along the way, we learn that he also never steals from neighbours and that he doesn't eat beef, none of which seems likely to secure him Avengers membership. However, 'He got subways in his teeth', so that's something.

Vambo the man might be a bit of an underachiever compared to the characters in Harvey's beloved Marvel comics, but 'Vambo' the song is a classic, one blessed with a joyous, singalong chorus and one of the Harvey Band's absolute best. In a just world, back when they built cars with CD players, 'Vambo' would have been a habitué of anthologies such as *Now That's What I Call Anthemic '70s Hard Rock That's Just the Ticket for Driving To*.

An aside: A quick peak on Amazon at a baker's dozen such compilations reveal that SAHB appear on a paltry three, with 'Boston Tea Party' gracing both *Top of the Pops: 70s Rock* and *Riding the Rock Machine: British Seventies Classic Rock*, and 'The Faith Healer' cropping up on *Classic Rock Anthems*. However, in today's Spotify World, there is no reason why Vambo can't now come to *your* rescue.

'Hot City Symphony Part 2: The Man in the Jar' (Harvey, H. McKenna, Cleminson)

Part two of the 'Hot City Symphony' begins with some wah-wah action that returns us to Isaac Hayes territory, specifically the *Shaft* soundtrack, which is appropriate as the narrative features an equally tough as nails if nameless detective. Hugh's piano overlay, reminiscent of the soundtrack to a Quinn Martin production, maintains the theme. Glen isn't the Man in the Jar, but he is the Man in Blue, the glue that holds it all together. Harvey's lyrics – 'I flipped open a packet of cigarettes and considered the situation' – reveal the protagonist to be of an older Chandleresque vintage. Lines like 'The fog drifted down over the river, and I turned up the collar of my coat' further confirm that this is indeed a homage to the Warner Brothers gangster flicks of his youth. This song, he told US DJs, 'represents an impression of New York'.

One of SAHB's unique selling points was that they went beyond the usual influences of the blues, Berry, and The Beatles, and tapped into a wider pop culture spectrum for inspiration. Movies, television shows, classic novels, pulp paperbacks, comic books, and music hall were all considered equally valid. The only contemporaries that came close to drawing from such diverse wells of creativity was the original Alice Cooper group, and they had imploded the year prior to *The Impossible Dream*'s release.

'There's a million sides to this band, a lot of things we can do', Harvey told the *NME* in 1974. 'It's a pretty good cowboy band – I don't mean C&W. It's also capable of being a very, very sophisticated nightclub band. And it can be a Deep Purple-type band. And it can get honky. There's no such thing as an audience not being our crowd. We're aiming at everybody'. This unconventional approach may have thrilled the SAHB's faithful, but in an industry reliant on labels – glam, prog, AOR – this idiosyncrasy likely also worked against them, as promoters, DJs, and even the record-buying public were never sure what they were going to get.

'The Man in the Jar', a '40s noir narrative backed in succession by '70s soul/funk, hard rock, big band swing, and a dash of scat jazz, all ably supported by an uncredited Big Bud's Brass, is the perfect song to demonstrate the futility of trying to pigeonhole SAHB. Best just enjoy the band's hard-boiled musicality and Harvey's lyrical adroitness. And, of course, there is a twist in the tale.

'River of Love' (Harvey, H. McKenna)
Another killer riff kicks this song off, but juxtaposed against it is Alex's gentlest, most accessible vocal on a SAHB song to date. It sounds as if he is mainstreaming his voice with a possible eye on some chart action, but 'River of Love' never received single release. Trying to second guess the fickle British public is a pointless exercise, but that memorable riff combined with some 'La la la-ing' that practically cajole the listener into singing along means this one, surely, could'a been a contender.

'Long Hair Music' (Harvey, H. McKenna)
All that stuff up above about SAHB drawing on a wide spectrum of pop cultural influences? The lyrics of this song throw such grand statements out the window, as the usually literate Harvey is reduced to writing the kind of 'fuck 'em, suck 'em' lyrics normally associated with Kiss. Okay, he is still way more playful than Simmons and company, but 'I gave my heart to Carmelita/ She's so groovy when I eata' isn't Alex at the top of his game. Let's cut him some slack and put it down to the tour-write-record-tour conveyor belt the band were well and truly on in 1974.

Fortunately, the band are up to the task, blasting out some serious white boy funk long before Wild Cherry played their funky music. It could be coincidence, of course, but the Ohio outfit's 1976 worldwide smash sounds heavily indebted to 'Long Hair Music'.

This song was originally called 'Can't Get Enough', which was also going to be the title of the album. Adverts even appeared in some of the trade press advertising the platter as such.

'Hey' (Harvey, H. McKenna, Cleminson)
This is a jokey jazz torch song that doesn't even make the forty-second mark and was the track that made people that only knew Harvey via SAHB gasp, 'Gosh! Alex can really sing!' Yes, he can, but it is Chris Glen playing the convincing crooner on 'Hey'.

'Sergeant Fury' (Harvey, H. McKenna, Batchelor)
One would perhaps expect a song named after Marvel Comics' tough-talkin', two-fisted World War Two hero to be some all hammer and tongs, heavy-duty hard rocker, but Harvey is having none of it, creating instead a 1940s swing number that builds upon the jazziness of the previous track. It is precisely the sort of tune one can imagine the fictional Fury listening to, perhaps as he enjoys downtime hobnobbing with high society in wartime London's Café de Paris, dancing to the sounds of Ken 'Snakehips' Johnson and His West Indian Dance Orchestra (Note: I'm evoking here, not being historically accurate).

One would also expect a song named after Harvey's favourite Marvel Comics hero to be about that character, but nope; the good sergeant makes a cursory appearance in the opening verse, the lyrics then becoming a clutch of random phrases much like those of 'Midnight Moses'.

Publicity in the music press optimistically touted this song as the 'best single ever', one that was 'released by public demand', but such sloganeering soon proved hollow when the record flopped. It was released on 20 July, the date the Harvey Band played the first-ever Knebworth Festival, and Alex jokingly told the crowd the festival was in honour of the single's release.

Curiously, Sergeant Fury's DC Comics counterpart Sergeant Rock also lent his name to a song title, 'Sgt Rock (Is Going to Help Me)', which XTC took to number sixteen in the UK charts in 1980.

'Weights Made of Lead' (Harvey)
Hanging as it does on five bluesy keyboard notes on nigh-endless repeat, 'Weights Made of Lead' might initially come across as, well, lightweight, but it is packed full of surprises: the vocal and guitar duet on the chorus, the surprise percussive pause, the vocal mid-section that briefly releases Hugh McKenna from his musical Mobius Loop, and, most of all, that weird guitar ostinato buzzing around the verse. That this is arguably the weakest track on the album only demonstrates how strong *The Impossible Dream* is.

'Money Honey'/'The Impossible Dream' (Jesse Stone/Mitch Leigh, Joe Darion)
'Money Honey' was Clyde McPhatter and the Drifters' debut single, released September 1953, and was clearly a favourite with rock and roll's first wave, being covered by Elvis Presley, The Coasters, Little Richard, and Eddie Cochran. On the Harvey version, Hugh McKenna and Cleminson whittle away at the primitivism of earlier readings by filling every available space, while Zal's fretwork and Alex's whisky vocals give the song a previously unheard grittiness. This is all well and good, but what elevates the track above mere filler is the masterstroke of pairing it with a snippet from 'The Impossible Dream', the standout song from the 1965 Broadway musical *Man of La Mancha*. For those doubting Thomases out there, this provides the album's second 'Alex can sing' moment, and this time it really is him.

That soaring, undulating penultimate delivery of the word 'star' is, dare I say it, sensational.

It will come as no surprise that Harvey, that great recycler of songs, used to perform 'The Impossible Dream' when he was adrift in mid-Sixties cabaret, but asked by *Melody Maker's* Harry Docherty why he revisited it now, he replied, 'It's funny. I like to have fun. There's no point in being, like, *this* is *my* art. I don't like that'.

'Tomahawk Kid' (Harvey, H. McKenna, Batchelor)

In the masculine world of '70s rock, a gay reinterpretation of Robert Louis Stevenson's classic novel *Treasure Island* was a tad bold and risqué, but bold and risqué was just another day at the office for the Sensational Alex Harvey Band. Still, one wonders if the crowds at such temples of machismo as the Glasgow Apollo knew what they were singing along to as they belted out, 'Let's be bold my captain, and I'll hold your hairy hand/And let's forget the treasure, and we'll skip across the sand'.

The source material is in no doubt as it is namechecked in the second line of the song, but Harvey being Harvey, this is a very loose interpretation of Stevenson's work. The Tomahawk Kid – a name possibly inspired by Marvel Comics stampede of similarly named western heroes (the Rawhide Kid, the Outlaw Kid, the Two-Gun Kid, etc.) – is Harvey's reinvention of the novel's central character, Jim Hawkins, and Billy Bones transitions from the novel unchanged, but the 'Captain Dan' named in the chorus is Harvey's own creation. The song's fourth character narrates events and is thus identified only as 'me', but it is a safe bet Harvey wouldn't exclude one of literature's more memorable villains, Long John Silver.

The song opens with some delicate piano from Hugh, Zal throws in a dash of Duane Eddy twang, and Chris and Ted join on the approach to the chorus. 'The Tomahawk Kid' is a relatively straightforward rocker, but it is full of little touches that ensure all buckles are swashed, such as the harmony vocals, some glam stomping from the rhythm section in the middle eight, the pirates' chorus on the fade, and Cleminson riffing like an alternative Vic Flick behind Harvey on the chorus.

'Anthem' (Harvey, H. McKenna)

Jazz, swing, funk, and rock have all coloured *The Impossible Dream's* ambitiously broad palette, but Scottish folk was another strand in Harvey's musical heritage, and it is to that he and Hugh McKenna turned for the album's epic closer, the appropriately named 'Anthem'.

Is 'Anthem' the first all-out Scottish rock song? It certainly wasn't the first to feature the bagpipes, that instrument cropping up in a diverse number of previous recordings such as Eric Burden & The Animal's 'Sky Pilot' (1968) and Parliament's 'The Silent Boatman' (1970), and Roy Wood gave the pipes a skirl on Wizzard's 1974 single 'Are You Ready to Rock'. Nor was it the first to lean on traditional Scottish music, that dubious honour going to Lord Rockingham's XI, who took 'Hoots Mon', a rocked-up novelty version of nineteenth-century jig 'The Hundred Pipers', to the top of the UK singles chart in 1958. 'Anthem' was, however, almost certainly the first rock song by a Scottish rock act built around an original piece of music that had Scottish folk – as opposed to rhythm and blues – as its base. As such it was a pioneering track, presaging the wave of 'Caledonian Rock' acts, such as Big Country, the Waterboys, and the Proclaimers, that enjoyed success from the 1980s on.

Ted McKenna gets things underway with a martial death march, the soundtrack of a tumbril trip to the guillotine. Plaintive female vocal-turned-soprano provided by Vicky Silva gives the tune a Celtic air, an impression reinforced by Hugh McKenna's equally melancholic piano. Hugh changes melody when Silva's vocals cut out, but the elegiac quality remains, and then Hugh too bows out as Alex sings the first verse, accompanied only by Ted, who alters his drum pattern but maintains the military flavour.

'Anthem' is a three-verse, chorus-free song that doesn't make a lot of sense lyrically, Harvey appearing to choose his words as much for their sound as their meaning. Thus, we get a wonderful example of sibilance in the couplet 'Telling stories to the peacocks/Selling systematically', and he relishes accenting the Glaswegian: 'Don't en-CURR-age me to MURR-dur'. Perhaps because he is only accompanied by the drums, Harvey utilises a greater degree of clarity during the first verse, and this further emphasises that 'Anthem' could easily be performed at a local folk music night without raising eyebrows. When the band join in on the second verse, he reverts to his familiar guttural vocal, taking glee in chewing every syllable, no more so than when he hits the 'systematically' mentioned above.

The second Harvey completes verse two's final line, Cleminson explodes into one of his finest solos, and one that encapsulates the entire song in that it is a rock solo inspired by folk. It surges above the other musicians, scattering a herd of deer as it roars up the mountainside where, upon reaching the snow-capped peaks, it soars into the sun-kissed blue on golden eagle wings. Okay, that's Scottish Romanticism rampant enough to punch its way out of a shortbread tin, but it is impossible not to picture Big Country's Stuart Adamson or Runrig's Malcolm Jones taking note of this solo in their teenage bedrooms, and that imagery is precisely what populated their videos the following decade. Even when Harvey picks up the third verse, Cleminson continues soloing away, busily filling every space with six-string wonderment whilst never distracting from the singer.

Alex, Zal and Chris drop out at the end of the third verse, and Hugh, Ted and Vicky Silva reprise the opening piece, which then builds when all five SAHBs join in on backing vocals, Chris and Zal resume their positions with Cleminson now echoing Hugh's keyboard melody, as do the pipers from the Pipes and Drums of the London-Scottish Territorial Army.

There was the loose-knit Celtic 'movement' of the 1980s that included the likes of Big Country, U2, The Waterboys, The Alarm, and Simple Minds, and the previous decade had a slew of acts not averse to letting their Celtic heritage shine, with Van Morrison, Thin Lizzy, Horslips, and Doll by Doll all springing to mind. Furthermore, the use of bagpipes on a rock song undoubtedly seemed old hat by the time Wings' 'Mull of Kintyre' ended its seemingly interminable run in the UK singles chart in March 1978. With this in mind, it is perhaps difficult to appreciate the power of 'Anthem' fifty years on, but in 1974 it was an absolutely thrilling piece of music. And, if truth be told, it still is today.

When 'Anthem' was released as a single in November 1974, *Disc*'s Ray Fox-Cumming said the song was 'much in the 'Amazing Grace' mould and just as powerful' and predicted that 'it should also be a huge hit'. He was right; it *should* have been a huge hit, but the best it managed was number 47 in the Australian chart. At nearly eight minutes long, perhaps it was too daunting for DJs, and perhaps Harvey was still considered too scary and his creepy clown sidekick too sinister for *Top of the Pops*; they could win over the crowd at Reading but not the readership of *Jackie*. 'Anthem' also got an American release, and it proved to be the band's Stateside singles swan song. Despite its lack of success, 'Anthem' remains one of the band's most essential tracks.

Vicky Silva, who provided the memorable soprano, was, like Harvey, a former *Hair* alumnus. She would later provide backing vocals on albums by Nazareth, Mick Ronson, Manfred Mann's Earth Band, and Everything But The Girl, as well as appearing as a singer in the house band of kid's teatime pop show *Get It Together* (1977-1981). As Victy Silva, she would go on to a successful career in musical theatre, television composition, and music education.

Tomorrow Belongs to Me – The Sensational Alex Harvey Band

Personnel:
Alex Harvey: vocals, guitar, harmonica
Zal Cleminson: guitar, vocals
Hugh McKenna: keyboards, synthesizer, vocals
Chris Glen: bass guitar, vocals
Ted McKenna: drums, vocals
Barry St. John, Liza Strike, Vicki Brown: backing vocals on 'Action Strasse' and 'Soul in Chains'
Derek Wadsworth: string and brass arrangements.
Produced at Scorpio Studios, London, by David Batchelor
Release Date: April 1975
Label: Vertigo
Highest Chart Place: UK 9
Running time: 37:15

The Sensational Alex Harvey Band were back touring the United States in March, mere months after the conclusion of their previous sojourn there. On one memorable date, 22 March, they supported Lynyrd Skynyrd at Johnson City, Tennessee, and were getting bottled by the crowd. In his autobiography, Chris Glen remembers Ronnie Van Zant striding on stage and telling the crowd to shut up. 'This is our favourite band', he told the audience, 'and if you don't like them, we ain't going on after them'.

In April, *Tomorrow Belongs to Me* dropped, just six months after its predecessor. The cover was again the work of Dave Field, based on ideas and images suggested by Alex. 'He explained it all to me', remembers Field in the *Last of the Teenage Idols* box set book, 'telling me about his idea of dinosaurs evolving into machines and trees dying of shame, the whole picture'. In his Harvey biography, John Neil Munro claims Field's cover 'parodied the trippy Roger Dean style artwork that Yes used to decorate their album covers in the 1970s', but Field makes no mention of that, and the *Tomorrow Belongs To Me* sleeve aligns with Dean's conceptual aesthetics more than it satirises them.

The ever-reliable Charles Shaar Murray called *Tomorrow Belongs To Me* 'a gorgeous mess', singling out 'Give My Compliments to the Chef' as the band's finest vinyl moment. Mick Houghton, writing for *Let It Rock*, said it had 'more light and shade (than previous albums), and the darkness is all the more impressive. Its place is the world of *Clockwork Orange* reality – of Vambo rule', concluding that it was 'more fluent and... is less diffusely structured than earlier albums. It has more compelling listenability'.

As with *The Impossible Dream*, press and public opinion coalesced, at least in Britain, where it became the band's first (and sadly, only) album to

10

crack the top ten, peaking at nine. By hovering around for ten weeks, it also provided SAHB with their longest chart run.

'Action Strasse' (Harvey, H. McKenna, Cleminson)

This song begins with Cleminson's guitar and Hugh McKenna's keyboards working in unison to simulate a gong, which kind of begs the question: why didn't Ted McKenna not just use a gong?

In comes Alex, singing that he wants 'to take a walk along Action Strasse', perhaps feeling nostalgic for his Hamburg days, when he played all-nighters at clubs like the Peppermint Shake mentioned in the lyrics. The streets in the song are populated with colourful characters like the 'one-eyed cat' and 'the painted lady' and there are always shady dealings going on: 'The man inside, he was selling me a bride'.

Tucked between the 'wanna take a walk' chants and the first verse is a lyrical seduction against a middle eastern interlude – music to charm snakes to – at odds with the German setting, after which the verse adopts a more familiar chugging rock groove. This Eastern influence is further emphasised in the coda, now accompanied by cries of 'Hey!' that owe more to Eurasian Steppes-dwelling Cossacks than the Glitter Band. The band could have played it straight and gone for the rock arrangement across the entire song, but their blending of three distinct musical styles over little more than three minutes demonstrates how adventurous they were creatively. Just for good measure, Cleminson throws in a second-generation glam solo *à la* Mott or early Sparks over the second half of the last verse, and one or all the backing trio of Barry St. John, Liza Strike, and Vicki Brown add some whispery Brides-of-Dracula-meet-Jonathan-Harker vocals under Harvey's lead.

'Snake Bite' (Harvey)

'Snake Bite' may be lyrically repetitive, but Harvey still squeezes out a touchingly romantic *bon mot*, 'She was the moon at night, the only light/That would ever brighten up my life'. Lovely, but then he blows it with the very next sentence: 'She was another man's wife'.

In many ways, this is a musical sequel to 'Long Hair Music' from the previous album in that weak lyrics are elevated by the band's muscularity. They reprise the funk of *The Impossible Dream* song, but here slather it in layers of sleaze in anticipation of Harvey's reveal.

'Soul in Chains' (Harvey, H. McKenna, Cleminson, Batchelor)

A bouncy bassline and some playful piano keep this song moving at a leisurely gallop behind Harvey's talking vocal. It's a soul song, but one initially performed as if SAHB were a club band on the chicken-in-a-basket cabaret circuit somewhere in northern England circa 1973, but the number grows in intensity, Ted's drumming becoming heavier with each verse, until Alex cuts loose vocally and the musicians suddenly transform into the Soul Band, circa 1963.

'The Tale of the Giant Stone Eater' (Harvey, H. McKenna)

If Harvey was found lyrically wanting on 'Snake Bite', then he more than makes up for it on this great big bewilderbeast of a song. 'The Giant Stone Eater' is more a surreal poem with musical accompaniment than a song, or a children's picture book illustrated by Dali.

While on holiday in the west of Scotland, Harvey came across once-unspoilt countryside being bulldozed to make a new road and 'The Giant Stone Eater' was his angry response. It is a non-linear, borderline stream-of-consciousness piece, but the basic gist is a riposte to man's destruction of the environment, condemning it both for its effect on the natural world, as referenced by broken antlers and trees dying of shame, and for its unwitting obliteration of history ('The eater... revs his mathematical rage/On the footprints of Vikings'). The titular giant stone eater is presumably the excavator seen on the album cover, and Harvey's warning is stark: if we don't take care of our planet, we will go the way of the dinosaurs ('Underneath a million tons of cold lava/A brontosaurus lies wrong way up').

Bizarrely, the lyrics of the song are apportioned to different characters – a Commentator, a Girl, a Man, or some combination thereof – but the voices of each are not distinct, and Harvey is the sole vocalist throughout, so the thinking behind this creative choice is unclear.

Musically... Jeez, where to start? The first thirty seconds alone contains solo voice, solo piano, five chords by the full band indicating the ominous approach of the titular stone eater, then some jolly nursey rhyme piano as Alex invites all boys and girls to gather round to hear his tale. Just beyond the thirty seconds, the tune suddenly sounds like a music hall number from the end of a 1930s pier, and just for good measure, there is also some soaring prog, some proto-industrial metal, and a good old hoedown thrown into the mix.

With all these shifts, 'The Tale of the Giant Stone Eater' can be tough going on first hearing. It is, as Chris memorably describes it in *SAHB Story*, 'ten songs in one, that disappears up its own arse'. But it is worth persevering with as it demonstrates both the versatility of the band all in one song, and Harvey's genuine concern for the environment long before it became a *cause célèbre*.

Harvey rated the song, telling *Melody Maker*'s Harry Doherty:

I don't listen to our albums. I can't bear to listen to them because there's always things that you think, 'I wish we'd done that.' There's only one track that I think we've ever done that I can bear listening to and that's 'The Tale Of The Giant Stone Eater'. I think that was a step forward. That was doing something new.

'Ribs and Balls' (Harvey, Glen)

Surely the owner of one of the world's most unappetising song titles, this is *Tomorrow Belongs to Me*'s space filler in the tradition of 'Hey' from the previous album, but is twice the length with half the charm. Chris Glen gets a nice bass riff going, one that would not sound out of place in Dr Feelgood's debut, *Down by the Jetty*, released in January that year, but the song never develops beyond that and ultimately the track comes across as little more than studio tomfoolery.

'Give my Compliments to the Chef' (Harvey, H. McKenna, Cleminson)
Like 'The Tale of the Giant Stone Eater', this is another wordy number backed by a brace of different musical styles. It starts with what sounds like the sonar pulse of a submarine which, three bleeps in, transforms into Glen's bass, after which Hugh and Alex join for a gentle first verse. The second verse brings in some Allman Brothers-styled southern blues, while the third recalls the heads-down boogie of Status Quo, that band so beloved by the *Bracknell Times'* Geoff Thompson. Live, it surely invited the audience to indulge in some serious headbanging, while simultaneously presenting them with a chorus that defied conjoining. Both Harvey and Cleminson were big fans of Frank Zappa, and the fourth verse recalls his avant-pop; indeed, the whole song could be described as Zappa-esque if one bears in mind his penchant for parodying popular music styles.

The title of the song was inspired by a real chef by the name of Mike Roydon, who had met the band in the Tear Gas days and again when SAHB were staying at the Liverpool hotel in which he worked, but the lyrics have little to do with a particularly fine meal. Taking the closing lines as a starting point, 'Go and take a look in a history book/Oh, it's up to you to mix the stew/And when you do/Give my compliments to the chef', it seems, as with 'The Giant Stone Eater', Harvey is issuing another warning. You can learn how to do the goosestep, he informs his audience, or you can join the Royal Navy, or, better yet, you can be aware that how you act now will write tomorrow's history. Write well, and tomorrow will belong to you.

'Shark's Teeth' (Harvey, Cleminson)
Can this really be, as the title suggests, about shark's teeth? Some couplets seem to be red herrings ('Jesus Christy was a mover/'Uncle see the highway keeper' – eh?), but this does seem to be about a shark, specifically a hammerhead, that gnaws on, in order, a railway sleeper, some piranha, a barracuda, and, most alarmingly, American actor Richard Widmark. And possibly Captain Cook, who, historically, did get eaten, but not by a shark. The shark then takes the protagonist of the narrative in its jaws, but he escapes by pushing its eyes in.

It is an odd lyric even for Harvey, the master of the odd. He was perhaps inspired by the novel, *Jaws,* which, upon release in February 1974, became an instant bestseller and topped the lists around the world. The film would be released a few months after this album

This takes us to the jazzy side of Funktown and is the first Harvey-Cleminson cowrite, and the guitarist peppers the song with wonderful phrasing and harmonics. Like the shark, the guitar in the intro is a killer.

'Shake That Thing' (Harvey)

Harvey returns to his blues roots, and what a slinky blues it is. The whole song is underpinned by a delightfully warm acoustic, presumably by Alex, while Zal adds some swampy electric over the top. 'Shake That Thing' becomes a party in song form when the rest of the band join in, and although there is no chorus *per se*, each verse ends with the couplet 'I told my story to the cannibal king/Said baby, shake that thing', presented here as the singalong equivalent of CinemaScope.

Speaking of couplets, one suspects Mr. Harvey was grinning ear-to-ear when he jotted down 'There's no such thing as a dirty book/It's just the way you read it' in his notebook.

'Tomorrow Belongs to Me' (Fred Ebb, John Kander)

In his liner notes for the 2002 Mercury release of *Tomorrow Belongs to Me*, Colin Somerville writes that the title track 'was a call to arms for Germany's brown-shirted youth in the Thirties, and in the liberal mid-Seventies even more non-PC than it would be deemed now'. In *All That Ever Mattered: The History of Scottish Rock and Pop*, Brian Hogg called the song 'a Nazi anthem'.

It was, of course, no such thing. Rather, it was a song written for the 1966 stage musical *Cabaret* by Fred Abb and John Kander, who were both Jewish, and popularised by the 1972 film adaptation. The musical is set in 1930s Germany, and 'Tomorrow Belongs to Me' is specifically introduced in the story to warn the characters that fascism is on the rise and that the days of the Weimer Republic are numbered.

In *The Sensational Alex Harvey*, John Neil Munro claims that the 'song had become a favourite of neo-Nazi sympathisers', and, surprisingly, considering the heritage of its composers, that was indeed the case. Perhaps they found it more tuneful than the awful oom-pah-pah of actual unofficial Nazi anthem, 'The Horst Wessel Song'.

With his background in musical theatre, Harvey would have fully understood the song's original context, but he was surely also aware of the then-current rise of the National Front in Britain, and that the inclusion of the song would have, as Munro says, 'raised some eyebrows'. However, Alex subverts the song by changing the 'me' to 'thee', effectively continuing the message begun on 'Give My Compliments to the Chef': learn from the mistakes of the past and write a better future.

'To Be Continued ... (Hail Vibrania!)' (Harvey, Cleminson)

Typical. You wait four albums for a Harvey-Cleminson song and two come along at once.

The SAHB boys must have been enjoying their funk because here is another in that vein, although the melody rings a bell. It's a fifty-second reprise of the 'Vambo' tune from *The Impossible Dream,* the lyrics first informing the listener that 'Vambo, he go on his way', before stating 'He come back some sunny day'. That last line sounds like a promise, so had there been talk of more Vambo songs or even a *Hail Vibrania* concept album? Cleminson: 'Alex had a notion to do something with *Hail Vibrania,* about a country where all citizens were allowed to commit two crimes and get away with them, regardless of their severity. The catch was if you committed a third crime, you automatically got the death penalty, no matter how trivial the offence was. But he never took it any further or offered a plan and it drifted into folklore'.

The Sensational Alex Harvey Band Live – The Sensational Alex Harvey Band

Personnel:
Alex Harvey: vocals, guitar
Zal Cleminson: guitar, vocals
Hugh McKenna: keyboards, synthesiser, vocals
Chris Glen: bass guitar, vocals
Ted McKenna: drums, vocals
Produced by David Batchelor from a recording at Hammersmith Odeon
Release Date: September 1975
Label: Vertigo
Highest Chart Place: UK 14
Running time: 46:15

The band undertook a 19-date UK trek promoting *Tomorrow Belongs To Me*, beginning on 1 May, with the show at London's Hammersmith Odeon on the 24th being recorded for a live album. Or was it? According to Chris Glen, talking to the *Glasgow Herald*'s Billy Sloan in 2021, the album was never meant for public consumption:

> We spent a lot of time on the road but never got to hear our show the way the audience did. We had no idea what we sounded like on stage. Our manager Bill Fehilly hired the RAK Mobile from producer Mickie Most to record the gig. It was a private thing. There was no plan for a live album.

This viewpoint is contradicted by Derek Nicol, interviewed for the *Last of the Teenage Idols* box set. 'In those days, we released two albums a year. The band were busy touring in Britain and America, so a live album seemed the natural thing to do'.

Meanwhile, Charles Shaar Murray reported on the Edinburgh gig for the *NME* and noticed a surprise inclusion in the set. 'No SAHB show would be complete without at least one totally surreal masterstroke (*à la* 'Man In The Jar' from the *Impossible Dream* show), and this time around, it's a thoroughly epic performance of Les Reed and Barry Mason's old Tom Jones chest-beater, 'Delilah''. Another notable gig, on 17 May, found SAHB at Stoke City Football Ground supporting Yes, with pseudo-medieval prog band, Gryphon, and pop rockers, Ace, also on the bill.

SAHB concluded their UK jaunt with an appearance on the *Old Grey Whistle Test* on 30 May, performing 'Give My Compliments to the Chef' and 'Delilah', and were then promptly off to the States for some scattered dates in June, returning the following month for a full tour supporting Jethro Tull. They were received, in the words of the seemingly omnipresent Murray, with 'bemused hostility' by fans of the headliners. 'Those fans who loved Jethro

Tull probably had a tough time figuring out SAHB in 40 minutes', said Janet Macoska, who had photographed the band and interviewed their frontman for her college newspaper the previous year. 'An audience needed more imagination to get into what SAHB was doing'.

Her feature on the band had opened doors for the fledgling photographer:

When the band came back a few months later, SAHB manager Bill Fehilly was with them. I shot the show at the Allen Theatre and came backstage to show Alex and Bill my article and give them some photos. Giant smiles on their faces. Bill was a giant of a man. He grabbed me in his arms and hoisted me off the floor and said, 'now you are clan'. And so I was. As I got to know Alex and the band (I also was hired to shoot publicity shots of the band in Louisville, Kentucky, during their Jethro Tull tour — my first paid gig!) I'd already been adopted as their photographer.

I asked her if she noticed differences between Alex Harvey, the performer and Alex Harvey, the man:

I'd had talks with Alex about the on-stage persona. I would describe it much as Alice Cooper having a different persona on stage. Alice Cooper is the character that Vince Furnier plays. Alex onstage is also a number of characters, because mostly he would feel that the songs particularly needed various personas to perform the songs. He was an actor as well as a performer. He once drew a sketch for me showing the audience sending all this energy towards him and he would give it back.

However, when Atlantic, SAHB's label in America, came up with a publicity stunt for a show in Cleveland, she saw a different side of Alex. The Music Grotto was the city's most popular record store, handily situated a block away from the Agora and across the street from Cleveland State University, the stomping grounds of the band's target market. Atlantic had bought one of the record store's walls for Harvey to 'vandalise' in front of the college audience.

He kind of freaked when it was told to him what he was supposed to do. He didn't know how to be his Alex character offstage, so I had to give him a pep talk, and explain what they wanted him to do, how it was just putting some graffiti on the wall with an audience watching. He was very uncomfortable about it. He did it, though. I felt bad that I had never expected him to feel this way and needed to get him through it for the record company and for the sake of the publicity. He wasn't prepared for this.

Alex the man was as intelligent and challenging as the fella onstage, and sometimes as dramatic (like playing Frankenstein with ten-year-old son Tyro in the middle of the night), but also pretty normal. We would go to the local park with his dogs and his two sons, wee Alec (who lived up in Glasgow with Papa and Nana) and Tyro. We'd watch the boys and dogs play (and I'd photograph them). We'd get ice cream at the kiosk. The most rock and roll thing we did was going to see Ian Dury and the Blockheads play in London.

As for the other band members:

Zal and Hugh were the quieter fellas, so I didn't get to know them that well. Ted and Chris were the two that were more outgoing. Like Alex, they didn't carry their onstage characterisations home with them. Zal, in particular, because of the makeup, could be much more outrageous onstage. I saw him when he played with Nazareth, and though he would pull a few Zal faces, he just worked the guitar so marvellously. He was and is a most awesome guitar player.

Meanwhile, back in Blighty, Vertigo released the live version of 'Delilah' from the May Hammersmith Odeon concert as a single, and by mid-August it had taken the Harvey Band into the UK Top Ten. For Alex, having a bonafide hit single must have been another moment of vindication: 'It's the greatest news I've ever had', he told the *Daily Record*. 'Having a top ten single is something you dream about. I never thought it would happen because I've tried so hard for so long'. It did, however, mean a transatlantic trip mid-tour so that the band could make their first-ever appearance on *Top of the Pops*.

Job done, SAHB were soon back in the US and on the road again with Tull. Two dates at Miami's Jai-Alai Fronton arena (28-29 August) proved memorable for the wrong reason when the band's equipment truck was stolen. Ted lost a snare drum that had been in the family since the 1940s, and Alex his pirate jacket, a leather jacket, and a Telecaster he had owned since his Soul Band days. Harvey made light of it, jokingly bemoaning the loss of two *Sgt Fury and His Howling Commandoes* comics, but the incident tarnished America for Zal: 'Sadly, my abiding memory of the USA is when our tour truck was stolen in Miami. I lost a pair of treasured Gibson SGs, a Marshall head and a 4x12 Vox cabinet'. Jethro Tull came to the rescue, lending SAHB their equipment and instruments, with Ian Anderson even lending Alex his black leather jacket to wear during 'Framed'.

The live album was at its zenith in the 1970s, being both an appealing concert souvenir for fans and an inexpensive way for record companies to pump out more product.Commercially successful concert documents already released that decade included offerings by the Rolling Stones, Deep Purple, The Who, Uriah Heep, Yes, David Bowie, and Lou Reed, so it seems inconceivable that the biggest-grossing live act in the UK would not follow suit. Regardless of the original reason for its recording in May, *The Sensational Alex Harvey Band Live* duly arrived at record stores in September and enjoyed seven weeks in the chart, peaking at 14. It was also the only SAHB album to trouble the American charts, if a one-week showing at number 100 can be defined as troubling.

Astonishingly, the band were back Stateside in October for the third time that year, when they shared dates with The Tubes, then touring their debut album. The Tubes had supplanted the now-defunct Alice Cooper group as the American act most like SAHB in terms of theatricality and diversity of musical styles, although the San Francisco outfit had an appreciably larger budget. The two acts alternated between support act and headliner on successive nights and meshed well, with Alex occasionally joining the other band on stage. Chris Glen must have gone down especially well with the Americans, as he states in his biography that The Tubes tried to poach him. SAHB also had a one-off date, 3 November, supporting Frank Zappa, which must have thrilled Frankophiles Chris, Zal, and Ted.

1975 was another triumphant year for the band, and one they were to see off in fine style with the legendary Christmas shows, three at the Glasgow Apollo (18-20 December) and three at London's New Victoria Theatre (21, 23, 24 December). The band had their most expansive – and expensive – stage set yet, a Glasgow tenement design with different levels and doors and windows that opened, and the band were on fire, but of course, what everyone remembers are the three dancers. They came on dressed for the ball in evening gowns, complete with opera gloves, during a performance of 'Cheek to Cheek', that old tune from the 1935 Fred Astaire/Ginger Rogers vehicle *Top Hat*. Once the song reached its middle eight, Alex directed each to spin in turn, revealing their backless dresses and their bare bums, each of which Harvey duly kissed. But, of course, you, the reader, already knew the punchline; *that's* how legendary those shows were.

In BBC Scotland's *Ex-S* documentary on Harvey, his widow Trudy saw these shows as the peak of the band's career, a sentiment Cleminson agreed with when talking to *Record Collector*: 'It's such a tragedy that it was never filmed. It was a massive production. It was the pinnacle of the band's performing life, in terms of theatrics, in terms of the choice of songs, the stage set and how we went about doing it all, with the dancers. It was just phenomenal, like a West End show'.

Returning briefly to *The Sensational Alex Harvey Band Live*, most of the songs have been covered in their respective studio entries, but it would be remiss not to pause and consider what Tim Barr, in the book accompanying *The Last of the Teenage Idols* box set, claims to be the album 'widely regarded as SAHB's finest hour on record'.

Credit for that must go not only to the band for their magnificent performance – and it *is* magnificent – but also to producer David Batchelor. The former Tear Gas frontman had been with the band since day one, first as sound engineer, then, from *The Impossible Dream* on, producer and co-songwriter, and *Live* is arguably his finest hour on record also. Here he is interviewed by Barr for the *Teenage Idol* box, and it is worth quoting him in full:

> It was very important to all of us that the band could go on stage knowing that, not only were they the greatest band in the world but that they *sounded* like the greatest band in the world, so we paid a lot of attention to that side of things. For me, the important thing, of course, was Alex's words. I knew the lyrics, the stories, inside out. It was crucial that the audience was able to hear every word he said. But because I've done the live sound from the beginning, been in the rehearsal rooms when the songs were being written, and been with them in the studio, I knew everything about every song too. I was working the faders all the time, making sure the audience got to hear everything as it was intended.

The result of this detailed working knowledge of the band and their material, and of Batchelor's ever-growing skill as a producer, means that *Live* is the single best album for truly appreciating the Harvey Band's superb musicianship. More so than on any studio album, the listener hears *every* drum skin Ted McKenna pounds and every cymbal he caresses; Hugh McKenna's reputation as a superlative musician is here justified, with every note ringing with resounding clarity; every incendiary chord Zal Cleminson lets loose burns with clarity; and Chris Glen, perhaps the player most buried in the studio mixes, emerges as the rock upon which the band is built. Live records are generally sonically muddier than their studio counterparts, but the opposite is the case here, and *Live* is an ideal starting point for anyone curious about the band.

Moving on to the songs themselves, the set opens with 'Fanfare (Justly, Skilfully, Magnanimously)', the Derek Wadsworth piece that played SAHB on stage each concert. It is a short piece, as full of fanfare as the title suggests, but hats off to The Harv for magnanimously including this on the record and thus ensuring some royalties for his old *Hair* mucker. Thereafter, the band launch into a proggier version of staple concert opener 'Faith Healer', a rousing 'Tomahawk Kid', and a truly thunderous 'Vambo', among others.

If *Live* has a drawback, it is one briefly alluded to above, and one that is solely down to their record label at the time, Vertigo. Deep Purple, Hawkwind, Traffic, and Barclay James Harvest are among those that preceded the SAHB into record stores with double live albums – Atlantic even stumped up for Yes to release the triple-live *Yessongs,* for crying out loud – and rather than running with a single disc for their boys, Vertigo should have gone the whole double hog. The *Teenage Idol* box finally rectified that wrong, and included the versions of 'Sergeant Fury', 'Gang Bang', 'Midnight Moses', and 'Tomorrow Belongs to Me' recorded at the same Hammersmith Odeon gig.

However, we end this chapter by turning our attention to that top ten single, which makes its album debut here.

'Delilah' (Barry Mason, Les Reed)

When Harvey and crew introduced 'Delilah' into their set during the 1975 British tour, they did so safe in the knowledge that most – if not all – of the audience would be familiar with it. It had been a huge hit for Tom Jones in 1968, peaking at number two (a position it held for three weeks) and remaining in the top forty for seventeen weeks. It became an instant favourite of cabaret performers, and Harvey himself was known to cover it in his late 1960s club gigs in London.

There is a reason Tom Jones is nicknamed 'the Voice' and his talent is undeniable, but his take of the song is a big band, Vegas-style production, with Jones finger-snapping away double-quick time as he delivers the lyric no differently from how he would 'She's a Lady' or 'What's New, Pussycat?'. A tale of the pre-meditated murder thus becomes a 'Housewives' Favourite', a right good singalong in the club, and panties were hurled in Tom's direction as he passionlessly slaughters a woman in song.

The SAHB version doesn't shake things up much musically, crucially retaining the flamenco-tinged flavour of the original, but as with 'Next', it is Harvey's delivery that drives the song. He is brooding, possibly boozy, and, as the lyric states, quite clearly 'out of his mind'. 'Delilah' is a murder ballad, but where the Jones version is focused on the second word, Alex voice-acts the role to emphasise the first.

This didn't prevent audiences from belting out the words at Harvey concerts of course, that Jones boy having set a precedent. And although the band might have performed 'Delilah' straight-faced, they didn't do it po-faced, as the choreography in the middle eight makes clear. For the uninitiated, this sees Chris and Zal dancing like Sylvester sneaking up on Tweety Pie before Alex joins them to display a trinity of wriggled arses.

As previously mentioned, the single cracked the UK top ten. Alex might have been delighted to have finally had a hit single, but Glen was concerned about possible repercussions. Speaking to *The Herald* in 2021, he said, "Delilah' reached number seven, but we were worried people might write us off as a covers band. We'd rather be known for 'Midnight Moses".

One can sympathise, especially when the band had already released some top-notch original 45s such as 'Big Louie', 'Jungle Jenny', 'Sergeant Fury', and 'Anthem', all of which the universe cruelly ignored. The band were not a covers band but rather a band that had recorded some cover songs amongst predominantly original material, as many other groups had done. Conversely, this point of view is weakened, at least in the eyes of the public, if all your studio albums to date have been named after cover songs, and when your next album is essentially going to be your version of *Pin-Ups*.

The Penthouse Tapes – The Sensational Alex Harvey Band

Personnel:

Alex Harvey: vocals

Zal Cleminson: guitars, vocals

Hugh McKenna: keyboards, synthesiser, vocals

Chris Glen: bass guitar, vocals

Ted McKenna: drums, percussion, vocals

B. J. Cole: Pedal steel guitar on 'Say You're Mine' and 'Cheek to Cheek'

Produced at Basing Street Studios, London, by David Batchelor

Release Date: March 1976

Label: Vertigo

Highest Chart Place: UK 14

Running time: 38:42

America's Bicentennial year dawned with no reason to doubt tomorrow still belonged to the Sensational Alex Harvey Band.

Things started promisingly enough, with an appearance on 6 February on *Don Kirshner's Rock Show*, with the host introducing them as 'a wild band from England'. The lack of songs from *Tomorrow Belongs To Me* suggests the recording occurred much earlier than transmission date, but the band were on form as they ripped through versions of 'Delilah', 'Vambo', and 'The Man in the Jar', with Harvey looking not unlike Peter Falk's crumpled detective Columbo when he donned hat and trench coat for the latter. It was only SAHB's second appearance on the American networks, but unfortunately, it would be their last. Even more crucially, the *Rock Show* appearance would prove to be the band's Stateside swan song; they would not play there again. Like T. Rex and Slade before them, and despite a few pockets where they had a fervent fanbase, SAHB ultimately failed to crack America. Janet Macoska has her own ideas about why this proved to be the case:

> Had MTV been in existence, I am totally certain they would have stomped all over America. America really didn't get a chance to experience this band. In the UK, or in other countries in Europe, there were music TV shows where the band could get nationwide exposure, but I believe that *Rock Concert* was the only TV show (shown at midnight) that the band appeared on in the US. There wasn't any unified radio to get behind a unique band like SAHB. They weren't mainstream rock like Bad Company or Peter Frampton, or whoever else was popular at that time. Furthermore, Mercury/Phonogram didn't put their full forces behind promoting SAHB but did put their promotional budget behind other acts on their roster. SAHB and their management knew that, which is why they moved over to Atlantic before the end of 1975 and came out with a live album, trying to capitalise on their live performance.

This being the case, I asked Janet why she thought SAHB were able to establish a beachhead in her native Cleveland and some other American cities:

Cleveland was a blue-collar city at the time. Working class. They worked in factories and as workers in various industries and rock and roll fuelled their lives. WMMS was the station everyone listened to, and we were able to hear music other stations weren't playing. We adopted many acts and made them our own. David Bowie's first US concert was in Cleveland, and Bruce Springsteen had his first popularity outside of Asbury Park in Cleveland. Roxy Music and others, the same. Cleveland identified with these Glaswegian guys, especially Alex. He was a superhero. Vambo. I suspect Detroit and NYC felt the same. We identified with this band because of theirs and our backgrounds, but also because their music was intelligent, humorous, in-your-face and real.

Nonetheless, tomorrow had begun to slip through their fingers. However, they were not to know that then, and the relentless rock 'n' roll show must go on. March saw the release of *The Penthouse Tapes*, their sixth album in just over three years. This was a collection of covers interspersed with three originals, although one of these was the 1973 single, 'Jungle Jenny', and another, 'Say You're Mine (Every Cowboy Song)', was a tune Harvey had been nurturing for 23 years.

Harry Doherty of *Melody Maker* claimed *The Penthouse Tapes* 'said very little', to which a defensive Harvey retorted, 'But I'm not tryin' to say anything. Everybody gets the wrong impression that I'm tryin' to say something or we're trying to say something. We're only a rock and roll band, we're not trying to say anything. The only thing I would ever say is, 'don't pish in the water supply.' That's all. What else is there to say?'.

Nonetheless, even the faithful Charles Shaar Murray labelled *The Penthouse Tapes* as 'the obligatory foolish pin-ups/favourite things cover versions and goof-offs (goofs-off?) scrapbook album', and in his autobiography, *The Bass Business* Chris Glen admits that '*The Penthouse Tapes* was a stopgap thing because we were too busy touring to have any product out. It wasn't a throwaway in terms of the music we had chosen, but it was a throwaway in terms of production – get in, get out, get it on sale'.

Another album begat another tour and beginning 30 April, SAHB trudged around the UK once more, this time with the Pat Travers Band in tow. May and June saw SAHB taking part in three stadium shows sold under the 'Who Put The Boot In' banner, at Charlton Athletic Football Ground (31 May), Celtic Park (5 June), and Vetch Field, Swansea (12 June). As the title suggests, the concerts were headlined by The Who, with the Harvey Band scoring second billing. Completing the line-up were Little Feat, The Outlaws, Streetwalker, and Widowmaker, an intriguing but short-lived 'supergroup' comprising Steve Ellis (Love Affair), Ariel Bender (Mott the Hoople), Huw Lloyd-Langton (ex- and future Hawkwind), Bob Daisley (Chicken Shack, Mungo Jerry), and

Paul Nichols (Lindisfarne). The Harvey Band were a late addition to the line-up but, it transpired, were vital in boosting ticket sales. Here's Chris Glen, interviewed in *SAHB Story*:

> Harvey Goldsmith, the promoter, wasn't sure it was going to sell out, so he looked for someone that would secure that. Until we were announced, Charlton had sold 17,000 tickets, after we were announced, it sold 51,000. I'm not saying we sold 34,000 tickets, but the idea of The Who plus Little Feat plus us made 34,000 people decide, aye alright, I'll go.

Harvey, who would regularly warn fans against vandalising venues and denounce rock 'n' rollers that wrecked hotel rooms, cautioned the famously destructive Keith Moon, 'Don't smash our gear, or I'll smash you'. This threat of violence was somewhat dwarfed by the actual violence that blighted at least two of the gigs. *Melody Maker*'s Chris Welch was at the Charlton show:

> All around, there were ferocious fistfights breaking out. Slugging combatants, incensed, perhaps, by a dig in the ribs, some spilt beer, or a blocked view, lashed out and kicked until parted by girlfriends or, in one minor battle, by a huge, red-coated security man with shaven head and gold earrings.
> It was a fascinating spectacle, far more riveting than the violence and silly antics of Alex Harvey, who pranced about as the gangster Hitler and then reminded cheering fans, who responded with raised arms, that the loveable old comic character so beloved of Charlie Chaplin was really 'a bastard' (Note: Welch gets it the wrong way round, or maybe Harvey did; it was Hitler who was a fan of Chaplin).

Welch appreciated the music more than the theatrics, calling 'School's Out' and 'Framed' excellent and stating the band 'displayed their grasp of dynamics' during originals such as 'Vambo' and 'Dance to Your Daddy', and noting that the band received a standing ovation. Also watching was vocalist/guitarist Henry Paul of Southern rockers The Outlaws, who probably inadvertently spoke for most of the United States when recalling SAHB for *Record Collector*:

> It was a very theatrical presentation, including scenery and various props. At one point, he was dressed up in a brown Hitler uniform, including a little moustache. Culturally, coming from where we did, I found his act to be odd, to say the least. As I recall, the crowd seemed into it and there was certainly no way to ignore it.

Despite Paul's bemusement and Welch's scorn, the Who Put The Boot In shows were a triumph for SAHB. The band were flying high as the scorching hot summer of 1976 dawned, but a fall was coming.

'I Wanna Have You Back' (Harvey, Cleminson)
This short but sweet little rock and roller is so tough its hair is slicked back with a stainless-steel comb. It features some T. Rex circa 'Get It On' guitar and makes for a solid, if slight, start to the album.

'Jungle Jenny' (Harvey, H. McKenna, Cleminson, Glen, T. McKenna, Batchelor)
It may have taken six people to write this song, but it was presumably Harvey that drew upon Edwardian adventure novels like *Rima the Jungle Girl* and female comic book Tarzans such as *Sheena, Queen of the Jungle* and *Jann of the Jungle* as inspiration.

Alex affects an Australian accent to introduce his own jungle heroine: 'This is a story I heard down in Wingo Wango/About a little girl called Jenny who got lost in the jungle/She was brought up by actual animals who lived in the bush/These apes got to like her so much the called her Jungle Jenny'. Quite why he chose to set it in Australia, a country lacking indigenous apes, is a mystery. No matter, Harvey is soon referencing fifties romance comics and their favourite trope of unrequited love, for Jenny has fallen for the lead singer of Willy and his Walnuts (at this point one would be forgiven for thinking high camp British television host, Larry Grayson, had a hand in the lyrics). Unlike the opening track, 'Jungle Jenny' has a narrative, although one missing a third act.

The Harvey Band were often pigeonholed as a glam act, but as previously discussed, it is better to accept them as unclassifiable. That said, 'Jungle Jenny' was originally released as a single three years earlier, during the height of the glam rock era, and it is probably the glitteriest song in the band's canon. It has the tribal stomp and shout-along chorus associated with Gary Glitter's biggest hits but maintains Mott the Hoople's grittier edge, and Zal's guitar sits somewhere between Mick Ronson's and Andy Scott's. It really should have been a hit.

Its resurrection in 1976 for *The Penthouse Tapes*, along with that of 'Runaway' and 'Cheek to Cheek' (see individual entries), indicates the thrown-together nature of this album.

'Runaway' (Del Shannon, Max Crook)
According to a *Sounds* review of a gig at the Greyhound in London in December that year, Del Shannon's 1961 global chart-topper formed part of the SAHB's repertoire as early as 1972, so it is perhaps no surprise they turned to it when under pressure to get a new album out. The result is a faithful reading of the original.

'Runaway' was released as a single in March '76, the third cover version in a row after 'Delilah' and 'Gamblin' Bar Room Blues' (of which more shortly). In the face of that simple statistic, one can understand Chris Glen's earlier concern about the band being perceived as a covers outfit.

SAHB made a promotional appearance on the 12 March edition of UK music show *Supersonic* to promote the single, during which Alex, Zal, and Chris abandoned any pretence about miming the song and premiered another nifty wee dance routine instead. It was another sterling example of simple, inexpensive, and remarkably effective theatre, and can be found on YouTube. Also abandoned for this appearance were Cleminson's green and yellow jumpsuit and Glen's Boy Blue look, with both wearing street rather than stage outfits (although Glen retains his codpiece and neckerchief). Whether planned or not, Cleminson's shorn hair, cropped-sleeve t-shirt and skinny black jeans mirrored the changing fashions that would soon have a seismic impact on the music industry.

Alas, the band's theatrics helped them not one jot and 'Runaway' stiffed.

'Love Story' (Ian Anderson)
A cover of a cover, with this version nodding more in the direction of Tear Gas's 1971 version than the Jethro Tull original. Midway through, Harvey switches to what could charitably be described as an experimental slant to vocal delivery, an approach he will apply to some of the other songs on this album.

'School's Out' (Alice Cooper, Michael Bruce, Glen Buxton, Dennis Dunaway, Neal Smith)
'School's Out' gave the original Alice Cooper group their international breakthrough in the summer of 1972, reaching number one in the UK in August – the only country it topped the chart – and cracking the top ten in Germany, Norway, New Zealand, and several others.

Harvey prefaces the song with an avuncular lecture like the ones he gave to gig-goers, even managing to fit in his oft-repeated advice about not pishing in the water supply, while Hugh provides a spectral fanfare, a slowed-down reading of the song's familiar riff.

Except for Cleminson ploughing a singular furrow on the solo, it is a relatively faithful take – enough so to render it the album's most redundant track – although Harvey goes OTT in his enunciation and delivery of the lyrics. He sounds like he might be trying a sinister Alice voice but only musters a sinister Alex instead, and school is blown to 'peeshes'.

'Goodnight Irene' (Lead Belly)
The acapella harmonies opening this Leadbelly standard and go-to song for supporters of Bristol Rovers are borderline exquisite, even if there is a whiff of collective tongues in cheek. Upon hitting the first verse, the band switch first to country, and then rocked-up country Jerry Lee-style, all played at a tempo undreamt of by the multitude who had previously committed 'Goodnight Irene' to tape.

As ever, Glen agilely anchors the song, and Hugh could grace any piano in Nashville's honky-tonk highway. There is a sweet denouement, as those opening harmonies return to supplant the instrumentation. This time it sounds ghostly, as if beamed in from a distant decade, the band approximating the Avalon Boys or their inter-war ilk.

'Say You're Mine (Every Cowboy Song)' (Harvey)

Alex keeps it country for this Hank Williams-styled ballad, and Cleminson effects a convincing slide guitar, but the clue is in the knowing subtitle; this sounds like every cowboy song you ever heard.

'Gamblin' Bar Room Blues' (Jimmie Rodgers, Shelly Lee Alley)

The main difference between the SAHB version of this song and Jimmie Rodgers' 1933 original is down to the number of players, as Rodgers performed his take accompanied only by guitar and harmonica. Alex also ditches some of the original lyrics and changes others, becoming more murderous when drinking with the policeman.

The band performed a memorable version of the song on 5 December 1975 edition of *Supersonic*, where, rather than mime the song as was custom, they acted it out instead, and in doing so, took their concept of cheap theatre to the max. Ted gets to be the flatfooted cop, sitting behind the wheel of his cardboard police car, and Hugh, looking like he wishes he was anywhere else, places his head above the cardboard body of the burly barman behind his cardboard bar. Poor Chris gets the short end of the stick, standing behind the cardboard body of a large-breasted woman, sporting a blonde wig and garish red lipstick, but given not a lot else to do. Alex and Zal act out a barroom brawl, and in accordance with the lyrics, Harvey brings a gun to a knife fight, after which he 'guns down' both Zal and Ted.

Despite this heroic effort, the single only just scraped into the top forty, reaching 38, although it did claim that 'coveted' number 44 spot for four weeks.

'Crazy Horses' (Alan Osmond, Wayne Osmond, Merrill Osmond)

Here the Harvey Band tackle another smash from the summer of '72, but one that raised more eyebrows than the Cooper cover. The Osmonds were never considered cool by any rock journalist anywhere, so when the inevitable question was asked, Alex would simply acknowledge that it was a good song. However, anyone remotely familiar with the singer would recognise that the song's ecological lyrics – the titular crazy horses are cars, and the song decries the pollution they cause – would resound with Harvey as much as its musical merits.

'Crazy Horses' is Zal Cleminson's *ex post facto* pick from *The Penthouse Tapes*, a surprise as he has been critical of many of the covers SAHB recorded. 'The whole album seemed unnecessary. Nothing we did really improved on the originals. I chose 'Crazy Horses' more as a compliment to the Osmonds' version'.

Curiously, the SAHB version of 'Crazy Horses' leaves out the original's most distinctive component, Donny's wailing Yamaha with portamento slide, replacing it instead with Alex inventing new syllables for the song title: 'Kuh-ray-ZEE Hor-SEZZ-uh'. Some tribal drumming from Ted eases into the tune proper, after which the band out-heavy the Osmonds' heaviest moment, and do so at a ferocious, ever-increasing tempo before culminating with a sudden and dramatic silence.

Harvey wasn't the only rocker that appreciated 'Crazy Horses'. Talking to Greg Prato for a 2021 *songfacts.com* interview, Donny Osmond revealed that Ozzy Osbourne told him 'Crazy Horses' was one of his favourite rock and roll songs.

'Cheek to Cheek' (Irving Berlin)
This straight reading of the Irving Berlin classic was recorded at the New Victoria Theatre, London during the 1975 Christmas shows, and was presumably included on *The Penthouse Tapes* to remind fans of those gigs' most unexpected moment.

SAHB Stories – The Sensational Alex Harvey Band

Personnel:
Alex Harvey: vocals, guitar
Zal Cleminson: guitars, vocals
Hugh McKenna: keyboards, synthesiser, vocals
Chris Glen: bass guitar, vocals
Ted McKenna: drums, percussion, vocals
Produced at Basing Street Studios and AIR Studios, London, by David Batchelor
and the Sensational Alex Harvey Band
Release Date: July 1976
Label: Mountain
Highest Chart Place: UK: 11
Running time: 37:15

In between touring, promoting *The Penthouse Tapes* and the stadium shows
with The Who, SAHB somehow found time to cut another album, and it was
heralded by the 'Boston Tea Party' single, released on 10 June. It put the band
back in the singles charts and, by being a band original, demonstrated that
they were more than just a covers act.

   The parent album, *SAHB Stories*, came out of the trap in July, and Murray
of the *NME* was back on side. 'Instead of jagged riffing framing declamatory
pronouncements', he wrote, 'we have seamlessly meshing music and vocals;
insidious rather than peremptory, incantation instead of declamation; mood
rather than props'. Good to know, but what does that *mean* exactly?

   It's a surprisingly mature performance – which implies no disparagement
   whatsoever of previous SAHB efforts – and a tremendously encouraging
   demonstration of the band's genuine growth.
      Dig: *SAHB Stories* is totally unlike anything Alex *et al* have done before.
      Even the sleeve symbolises the changes within: The 'Sensational Alex
   Harvey Band' logo, which has graced the sleeve of all seven of their previous
   albums, has been ditched, as has the garish comic-book art style.
      The ringmaster/circus relationship that Alex has had with the band
   on previous recordings has been rebalanced; Mister Harvey now sings
   from *within* the band (who, incidentally, play like sensuous bulldozers
   throughout).

Safe to say he liked it then, as did the British record buyer, who sent it to
number eleven, SAHB's second-highest chart placing. And, as Murray points
out, this was the first album not to display Dave Field's classic band logo,
which would be reinstated for all subsequent releases.

   Looking at the record from a near-fifty-year distance, Zal Cleminson still
regards it with fondness. 'It's a very polished album, with a number of good
songs, all of which highlight the band's musical versatility'.

So far, so 1975, which in turn was 1974's near twin. Record. Tour. Promote. Repeat, gaining incrementally each time. But then came 27 July 1976, a lovely sky-blue day, another of the endless many in the heatwave that would sear its way into Britain's consciousness. But for the Sensational Alex Harvey Band, it was the day that marked the beginning of the end.

Manager Bill Fehilly was flying from Blackpool to Perth when the Piper Aztec aircraft he was travelling in crashed into Great Hill, seven miles northeast of Moffat in Dumfries and Galloway. The subsequent inquiry concluded that pilot Eric Scott lost control when the left engine failed due to a severe oil leak, and the plane rapidly lost altitude and smashed into the hill. The resulting inferno reduced the plane to ashes and claimed the lives of all six people on board, including Bill's eleven-year-old son Liam. The remaining three victims all worked for Fehilly's Top Flight company.

Fehilly's passing had a crushing impact on the band, both from a personal and business point of view. In *The Bass Business*, Chris Glen recalled, 'The whole thing was absolutely devastating. Bill had been Alex's mentor, so Alex didn't take it well at all. And Alex was my mentor, so it went down the line.' Zal, in *SAHB Story*: 'We were stunned – everything ground to a halt. And of course, it knocked Alex for six'.

Talking to *Mojo* in 2000, Harvey's son Alex Jnr. was unequivocal regarding the impact Fehilly's death had on his father. 'Where the end of my dad's life is concerned, look no further than Bill's death to understand the whole thing. He couldn't cope with it'.

Ted McKenna, in *All That Ever Matters*: 'Bill was a warm-hearted, charismatic guy and was the only person who could handle Alex. When he died, it was like the sun going down, it was a big blow to Alex, but that's when we realised the management didn't know what it was doing, at our expense. We lost a lot of money playing in America, no-one was taking care of business'.

Bill and Liam Fehilly's funeral was held in Perth on 4 August, with SAHB – including a clearly distressed Harvey – and members of Nazareth in attendance. The following day the band were in London for a meeting with Mountain Records, after which Harvey was interviewed by Phil McNeill of the *NME*. 'He (Fehilly) was the only man I could call captain, Phil, he was my blood brother. But we're going on and Mountain's going on'. Two days later, the band were in Finland, sharing the bill with Chuck Berry at the Ruisrock Festival.

Later that month, while speaking to *Melody Maker*, Harvey expressed his belief that change was coming. Talking about the current music scene, he said: 'It's got straight. It's got really, really straight. Muzak. It's exactly the way it was in 1956 when it was 'How Much Is That Doggie In The Window' and stuff like that, and then suddenly Elvis came bustin' through and it was like a breath of fresh air. And that's what it needs now. I don't think it's us. It'll be some young kids somewhere'. Although he wouldn't have been aware of it, the 'young kids' were already gathering, as just a month earlier, on 4 and 6 July, two newly formed bands, The Clash and The Damned, supported the not-much-older Sex Pistols. The 'breath of fresh air' that Harvey predicted was already on its way.

SAHB toured Europe in the autumn, a territory largely neglected in their attempts to crack America. All was well initially, Alex outrageously sporting his Hitler moustache while performing 'Framed' in Germany, but his behaviour grew increasingly erratic. In Malmo, he fell asleep at the microphone and then pursued Cleminson with murder in his eyes when the guitarist gave him a kick to wake him up. At other times he had to ask, mid-song, what the lines of the next verse were, even when performing concert staples like 'Delilah'. On another occasion, he left the stage while Zal was performing a solo, and then refused to go back on. Ted McKenna had to cajole the singer to return, using Alex's own 'man up' tactics against him. Harvey complied, but, as McKenna remembers it, 'he kept whimpering that he didn't want to be there anymore'.

Things came to a head in Lund, Sweden, on 7 October. Harvey felt ill during the show and took a short break before feeling well enough to continue. Once the concert was over, however, he collapsed. The rest of the tour was cancelled, and Harvey flew back to Britain the next day to recover. Grief, total exhaustion, depression, and a vodka bottle-a-day habit had taken its toll.

'Dance To Your Daddy' (Harvey, H. McKenna, Cleminson, Glen, T. McKenna, Batchelor)

The SAHBs had by now repeatedly demonstrated that they were white boys that *could* play that funky music, but for any lingering doubters, here's 'Dance to Your Daddy'. However, this is more polished and shinier, a slick floor filler that's not quite slick enough for disco and considerably less urban than their previous saunters into the genre. Harvey even dials the 'Glesga' down and out of existence and sings like he is auditioning for American radio. And perhaps he is, he and the boys blissfully unaware that at the time of writing and recording, Alex's Adventures in America were over.

None of which detracts one iota from 'Dance to Your Daddy' being a strong album opener, and that's even without accounting for the dreamy lullaby of a coda, wherein Hugh emulates tweeting cartoon bluebirds, that cutesy little breed that habitually sang to Snow White or Mary Poppins, to bring the song to a sweet and surprising conclusion.

'Amos Moses' (Jerry Reed)

This is a swampy Southern gothic blues number that Mountain Records decided had 'hit record' written all over it. It didn't. Perhaps it might have gained some traction in the States, but it was never released there, and anyway, the Jerry Reed original, a number eight pop crossover hit in 1970, was surely still too fresh in the memory. In a Britain where rock and prog still reigned supreme, where punk was lurching awake, and where acts such as Tina Charles, Candi Staton, and Abba were ushering in the disco era, a slice of swamp blues stood no chance of being noticed. And fair enough, for SAHB, those great interpreters of other people's material, fail to rise above the pedestrian with this one, or perhaps the song itself was simply no great shakes to begin with. Either way, they shoulda danced with her daddy instead or gone for the 'Jungle Rub Out'; they may or may not have been hits, but both would surely have had a better shout at some all-important airtime.

'Jungle Rub Out' (Harvey, H. McKenna, Cleminson, Glen, T. McKenna, Batchelor)

Chris Glen's muscular bass gives this song its first breath, with Cleminson soon contributing a soft, scratchy counterpoint, before Hugh McKenna's gossamer-light flute-like synth sends it soaring. It sounds as if the SAHBs are heading into prog territory before reconsidering and setting sail for the newly polished funk established in 'Dance to Your Daddy'.

Having been absent on the preceding two tracks, the Glaswegian sneaks back into Harvey's voice, but it is an accent with aspirations of moving to the city's bohemian West End. Perhaps he is just trying to keep it radio-friendly.

And since we are in 1976, I can say things like 'dig that chorus'. Such an infectious thing it is, beckoning the listener to join in, and how could they resist? 'Down in the jungle, doin' the rub out', sang the faithful, with neither clue nor care what the hell they were singing about. What need had they of that, when that well-placed double handclap on the comma spurred them so joyously along.

'Sirocco' (H. McKenna)

'Sirocco' is a unique entry in the SAHB catalogue, being composed solely by Hugh McKenna and therefore, as the *Last of the Teenage Idol* box set book points out, 'the only occasion that one of the band members wrote words for Alex'. 'I was very proud of the fact that he had done a lyric of mine', McKenna told author Tim Barr. 'Alex actually told me 'I tried to improve on it, but it is perfect as it is', which I took as a great compliment'.

Cleminson gets things going with some slow blues guitar, but not surprisingly, it is McKenna who dominates the song, steering it away from the bayou and the blues and into the desert. It is full of little Middle Eastern flourishes, most prominently the repeated refrain from a synthesised choir that subs as a chorus, and McKenna uses his keys to conjure forth the wailing animals mentioned in the lyric. Hugh also does a nice job shadowing Harvey's lead vocal by pitching his own voice an octave higher.

'Sirocco' is the longest song on the album and unfolds at a languorous pace, but it effectively builds mood and atmosphere and slips away like a sidewinder before overstaying its welcome.

'Boston Tea Party' (Harvey, H. McKenna)

The Boston Tea Party was an anti-tax protest conducted in December 1773, in which members of the Sons of Liberty organisation boarded three ships belonging to the British East India Company and dumped their entire cargo of tea into Boston harbour. The demonstration was considered an act of treason by the British government, who responded harshly, and the incident was one of the events that ushered in the American Revolution, which ultimately resulted in the United States gaining independence from the United Kingdom. It was, therefore, highly topical song material in 1976, the year in which the US celebrated the Bicentennial of its independence.

Noel Edmunds knew this when, sporting a tie wider than his face, he introduced the band's first performance of the song on *Top of the Pops* on 10 June. 'Now here's a song that's rather appropriate for Bicentennial year', he told the viewers at home, 'a little bit of a history from the Sensational Alex Harvey Band and the 'Boston Tea Party''. Tony Blackburn was equally aware of the song's topicality, making the link to the Bicentennial plain during the band's next *TOTP* appearance a full month later on 8 July.

Surprisingly, the band had to push for 'Boston Tea Party' to be released as a single, the record label seemingly unaware that a song tying in with one of the big news events of the year might have commercial value. The madness at Mountain, with apologies to H. P. Lovecraft. Of course, SAHB were vindicated, as the single became their most successful, charting stubbornly for ten weeks, twice dropping and twice rising again. It peaked at 13, six places lower than 'Delilah' the previous year, but its extended chart run meant it sold more copies.

The song had its genesis at Chris Glen's house, when Harvey called Hugh McKenna aside and asked him to play whatever he wanted while Alex sang the lyrics over a soft tribal drumbeat. As the singer related the historical circumstances for America's preference to coffee over tea, Hugh played an equally gentle set of cyclical chords starting with a C sharp minor. McKenna's playing is both inspired and sublime, and, along with Harvey's history lesson and the falsetto backing vocals, is one of the tune's defining characteristics. Cleminson's guitar solo was edited out of the single version to meet some esoteric criteria defining what constitutes a pop single.

Speaking of defining, the chart success of 'Boston Tea Party' means it is the self-composed song the casual listener most associate with the band, but at least, unlike, for example, Warren Zevon and 'Werewolves of London', it also happens to be one of their very best. It even had fans in high(ish) places: according to songfacts.com, Sarah Ferguson, Duchess of York, selected 'Boston Tea Party' as one of her favourites during a BBC daytime radio show.

'Sultan's Choice' (Harvey, Cleminson)

'Sultan's Choice' is the first straightforward rocker on *SAHB Stories* and is driven primarily by Cleminson's insistent riffing and some truly thunderous drumming from Ted McKenna. It rattles along at a furious pace, pausing only for a middle eight that draws upon the same Sixties soul and R&B influences that propelled the Beatles' 'Taxman' a decade earlier.

Lyrically, there are all sorts of Egyptian shenanigans, with references to Cairo, the Nile, belly dancing, and pyramids, but there is also this curious couplet, 'Even if a man is pure of heart/And he says his prayers by night'. This betrays Harvey's love for Hollywood's Golden Age, as it quotes the snippet of 'old European folklore' originally written by Curt Siodmak for the 1941 Universal horror movie *The Wolf Man*. Siodmak's follow-up line is 'May become a wolf when the wolfsbane blooms and the autumn moon is bright', and ill befits Alex's Amorous Adventures in the Land of the Pharaohs. Perhaps he should have opted for quoting Universal's *The Mummy* (1932) instead.

'$25 for a Massage' (Harvey, Cleminson, Glen)

That predominant plump thumping bass and effervescent guitar riffery inform the listener that Glen and Cleminson are the co-authors of this track without resorting to reading the credits (it is also Cleminson's favourite track off the album). It is 1976, the year the American funk-rock-soul band, War, were at the height of their commercial success, and going by the number of funk-rock tracks on *SAHB Stories*, it appears the Glaswegians were trying to give the Californians a run for their money.

'Dogs of War' (Harvey, H. McKenna, Cleminson)

'Dogs of War' was inspired by the Frederick Forsyth novel of the same name and was, according to Harvey in an *NME* interview (21 August 1976), a 'fierce put-down of mercenaries'. The timing might be slightly off, but another inspiration may have been the Luanda Trial, the trial of thirteen Western mercenaries (nine Britons, three Americans and one Irish) in Luanda, Angola, which resulted in four of the men facing the firing squad and the others receiving long-term prison sentences. Although the trial took place in June, a mere month before *SAHB Stories* was released, the mercenaries were captured in mid-February, and the story may have caught Harvey's eye.

'Whosoever touches one hair on yon grey head', announces Harvey in the opening proclamation, 'dies like a dog. March on!' For a moment, he has forgotten that he is on a mission to seduce American radio, so Glaswegian Al is back in all his guttural glory, and 'grey' is 'GRRR-ey'. In comes the band, Cleminson dishing up some heavy metal on the guitar, a nice counterpoint to a softly singing Harvey, who has remembered his Received Pronunciation. By the third verse, Harvey has abandoned comprehension entirely, going for a 'mad drunk braying in the street' approach instead, his dialect more gonzo than Glasgow, and as we leave him – and the song – he appears to be howling at the moon. Perhaps it was because he got to cut loose on 'Dogs of War' that Harvey named it as his pick of the *SAHB Stories* bunch.

The Harvey Band, meanwhile, demonstrate their penchant for changing musical styles over the course of the same song, as the in-your-face verses give way to something altogether more pastoral at the chorus, ethereal folk rock perhaps, its dreaminess contrasting with the rawness of what came before.

Related Songs
'Satchel and the Scalphunter' (Harvey, H. McKenna)
This oddity appeared on the flip side of the 'Amos Moses' single, and lord knows why, as it is truly awful. Narrated as if talking to a class of primary one kids rather than sung, with Hugh providing some piano to skip to, a little girl called Satchel – so named because she has a satchel – encounters Dutch Druid and the Elders. Apparently, these are 'very naughty boys with a dreadful reputation for leering and looking at little girls skipping along the road', so she phones up her chum Scalphunter who comes along and gives Dutch and the Elders an overclose shave.

Perhaps I should have thrown up some spoiler alerts before telling you how it all ends, but I like to think I listened to this drivel so that you don't have to.

Fourplay – The Sensational Alex Harvey Band Without Alex

Personnel:
Hugh McKenna: keyboards, lead vocals
Zal Cleminson: guitars, vocals on track 5
Chris Glen: bass guitar
Ted McKenna: drums, vocals on track 4
Produced at Basing Street Studios and AIR Studios, London, by John Punter and the Sensational Alex Harvey Band (without Alex).
Release Date: February 1977
Label: Mountain
Highest Chart Place: Did not chart
Running time: 36:12

With Harvey under doctor's orders to rest, there was no possibility of a new SAHB product, but that didn't stop Mountain Records sending the band into the studio to make an album billed as SAHB (Without Alex). Punningly entitled *Fourplay*, this would consist of songs primarily written by Hugh and Zal that they either considered unsuitable for SAHB or had been floated and knocked back. According to Cleminson, the album 'offered a chance to express ourselves in a different light, and to be more technical in our approach'.

John Punter was the man occupying the production booth. He had previously been behind the console for Roxy Music's *Country Life* (1974) and for the 1976 debut from Doctors of Madness, and would go on to produce some of Japan's defining albums, as well as working extensively with SAHB's old tourmates Slade in the 1980s. Another regular visitor to the studio was Harvey himself, who showed up to offer encouragement and scotch press rumours that SAHB were on the verge of splitting. He even appeared on the back cover of *Fourplay*.

On 20 January 1977, the band (without Alex, natch!) appeared on *The Old Grey Whistle Test* to preview the album, performing 'Pick It Up and Kick It' and 'Smouldering'. Just as he had done for the album cover shoot, Cleminson ditched his trademark whiteface and jumpsuit for the show and looked comfortably new wave amongst the longhairs. His bandmates had also discarded their usual SAHB attire, with even Glen's blue codpiece M.I.A.

On 26 January, they set off on a nine-date UK tour, playing the college circuit and other venues smaller than those they had become accustomed to. The set list consisted of the *Fourplay* album in its entirety, a cover of Bowie's 'Stay', and just two SAHB tracks, 'Jungle Rub Out' and 'Delilah', which they played as an instrumental and encouraged the audience to sing.

The album was released in February, as was *Alex Harvey Presents the Loch Ness Monster* (see below), but both sank without trace. There was a third

SAHB-related album in 1977, with May seeing the release of the band's first-ever compilation *Vambo Rools: Big Hits and Close Shaves*. Like many a jilted record company when a band departs for pastures new, Vertigo decided to cash in on SAHB's continued success and issue a 'best of'. Despite its title, however, there is a distinct lack of 'Vambo', only one big hit ('Boston Tea Party' is excluded as it came out on Mountain), and 'Gamblin' Bar Room Blues', the band's only 'close shave', is nowhere to be seen.

'Smouldering' (H. McKenna, Glen)
Much of the Harvey Band back catalogue benefitted from Hugh McKenna's fine harmony vocals, but did he have what it took to graduate to lead singer? Not really, is the answer. On the one hand, his pipes are polished enough to fit with the west coast prog meets white boy soul vibe of the opening track, but on the other, well, 'polished' is just another way of saying nice. It *is* a nice voice, undoubtedly technically proficient, but it doesn't possess enough character to be particularly memorable.

For a song credited to Hugh and Chris Glen, the deportment of the players is interesting, the composers happy to let Ted and Zal lend the song its heft while their airy playing adds the poise.

'Chase It Into the Night' (H. McKenna, Cleminson)
This song blasts off with some serious boogie-on-down guitar of the kind favoured by 'the Quo', but any fears we are heading into Heads Down Land are allayed when Hugh comes in with a barroom-ish keyboard motif which is languid to the point of discordance, and would probably have Frank Zappa nodding his arched-brow approval.

'Ah', sayeth the nonconformist who bequeathed his name to a moustache, 'I see where you are going here', and he would be most definitely wrong, because SAHB(WA) change tack again and invent Toto a full eight months before Toto did. And no one saw that coming.

'Shake Your Way to Heaven' (H. McKenna, Cleminson)
This song makes it the third in a row that confirms the band were using their newfound freedom from their bee-striped boss to try out some sophisticated AOR in the Doobie Brothers or Supertramp mould. 'Pick It Up and Kick It' was the only single released from *Fourplay*, but 'Shake Your Way to Heaven' would also have made a catchy calling card.

'Outer Boogie' (H. McKenna, T. McKenna, Cleminson, Glen)
Ted McKenna takes over lead vocals on 'Outer Boogie' and hits a particularly impressive high note round about the 2.15 mark. There is some screaming, echo-heavy guitar from Cleminson, lovely Moog soloing in the middle eight, and the rhythm section maintain a smooth funk groove throughout, but one more aligned to Steely Dan than the Family Stone.

'Big Boy' (Cleminson)

The band indulge in a game of Pass the Microphone, and Zal is left holding it when the music stops. The crunching guitar intro is reminiscent of Manny Charlton from labelmates Nazareth, and although Cleminson lacks Dan McCafferty's range, there is a definite hint of the Naz's frontman in Zal's delivery. Perhaps it should come as no surprise then that when Zal later joined Nazareth, they recorded 'Big Boy' for their *Malice in Wonderland* (1980) album. The Naz version has a distinct reggae feel, possibly inspired by being recorded at Nassau in the Bahamas.

Such an influence is entirely absent from the SAHB(WA) original, but there is the delightful counterbalance between the rock-hard verses – during which Hugh's keyboards are neatly tucked behind the guitar – and the delicate, keyboard-driven chorus with ghostly backing vocals.

A restrained solo from Cleminson leads to the conclusion consisting of the band singing a mantra of 'What a Night/You can have', during which the former clown face finally encourages his guitar to shed its inhibitions. The excellent fretwork aside, this section is arguably too long and repetitive, and the song would have benefitted more from an abridged verse and third chorus, but even with this, 'Big Boy' remains the highlight of the album. What the lyrics are about is anybody's guess, but this could have been another possible single.

'Pick It Up and Kick It' (H. McKenna, Cleminson)

The album's sole 45, 'Pick It Up and Kick It' is a big, bluesy pub rocker with a healthy dose of funk, and demonstrates the sheer musicality – and muscularity – of the band more than any other *Fourplay* track. The rhythm section is immense, Ted terrific behind the kit, a drummer's drummer, and Glen's bass a thing of fat, pulsing joy. Zal gets in some guitar hero licks, but Hugh takes the honours with his splendid soloing and his single-best lead vocal. Got some cobwebs that need to be blown away? This song will take care of it.

'Love You for a Lifetime' (H. McKenna)

This mid-tempo ballad is by some distance the poppiest song on the album and sits somewhere between early '70s Marmalade and the theme tune of some '80s/'90s American sitcom. 'Love You for a Lifetime' sounds as far removed from the rest of the album as the rest of the album does from the band's output with Alex, and suggests that Hugh, the song's sole writer, had a greater commercial leaning than his bandmates.

'Too Much American Pie' (H. McKenna, T. McKenna, Cleminson, Glen)

Everyone piles on to write this one, and it may just be a case of too many cooks spoiling the pie. Zal writes some great guitar parts and Hugh produces stellar work, especially on the extended fade, but no one seems to have brought along a tune. Ultimately, this sounds like something they wrote in the hope Foreigner would offer them a job. However, it's Zal's pick o' the album, so what do I know?

Alex Harvey Presents the Loch Ness Monster – Alex Harvey

Personnel:
Alex Harvey: interviewer, narration.
Richard O'Brien: narration
David Batchelor: field recording
Leslie Harvey Snr: research
Produced at Point Studios, London, by David Batchelor and Alex Harvey.
Release Date: February 1977
Label: K-Tel
Highest Chart Place: Did not chart
Running time: 41:18

Easily the oddest album in the Harvey canon, *Alex Harvey Presents the Loch Ness Monster* is also arguably the weirdest release by any mainstream rock star, with the possible exception of Lou Reed's 1975 headscratcher, *Metal Machine Music*. It is not a concept album, as the title may suggest, but rather a documentary, and although there are seventeen tracks, it is best to view the album as a whole.

But first, some background. Harvey and family headed to the shores of Loch Ness for some well-deserved downtime in the scorching July of '76. Some much-needed rest was on the cards, but, having been intrigued by the loch's famous inhabitant since he was a child, Harvey fancied his hand at a spot of monster hunting. Thanks to the publication of Robert Rines's famous 'fin' and 'gargoyle' photographs the previous year, 'Nessie-mania' was at an all-time high that summer, and Alex planned to interview some locals that claimed to have seen the elusive beast. His father acted as the advance scout, and Leslie Snr. had a stream of interviewees lined up for his son's arrival. Along with wife Trudy, children Alex Jnr. and Tyro, and family dogs, the party included David Batchelor and his assistant Tam Fairgrieve, who would record proceedings.

Against a backdrop of whale song and submarine sonar, the album opens with a forty-second introduction by Richard O'Brien of *Rocky Horror Show* fame, before moving onto local policeman Sgt Nicholson who gives the first part of his encounter with the monster. The bells of Fort Augustus Abbey then ring out, introducing the listener to Father Gregory Brussey, who gives an account of the oft-told apocryphal first sighting of the monster, by Saint Columba in the River Ness in 565 CE, which Brussey is quick to dismiss as mere legend. Hurrah! It seems Alex is wisely imbuing the project with a healthy degree of objectivity, but no, for now, Father Brussey is recounting his own sighting.

And on it goes, one eyewitness account after another, and although Harvey handles his role as interviewer well, and tries to instil some cod-gravitas

('Sitting in a room full of history sipping sherry, Mrs Grant began her story') it appears he is only interested in the Nessie yesses. There is no room here for counterargument, or, heaven forbid, science. Alex even interviews Frank Searle, a dedicated Nessie-spotter of seven years at the time, but one that had already been debunked as a persistent hoaxer in future BBC journalist Nicholas Witchell's *The Loch Ness Story* (1975). Better still – or worse, depending on one's point of view – is the inclusion of Alex Campbell, who recounts the first of his many sightings. 'That was Alex Campbell', states Harvey in obvious admiration, 'who was water bailiff on the loch for nearly forty years. He should know'. Indeed yes, he *should* know, and more than most, for according to hysteria-free books about the monster, such as *The Loch Ness Mystery Solved* (Binns, 1984) and *A Monstrous Commotion* (Williams, 2015), Alex Campbell is the rogue who single-handedly engineered Scotland's greatest hoax by essentially inventing the Loch Ness Monster.

The album concludes with its only song, 'I Love Monsters Too', a Harvey original that struck a chord with Peter Silverton of *Sounds*:

Even if you hate all-talking records, even if you couldn't give a damn about the story of Nessie, you've got to admit that the album contains, in 'I Love Monsters Too', one of the sweetest, finest lullaby sing-alongs you've ever opened your ears to. Alex Harvey as wide-eyed nursery school innocent might boggle your mind, but there's no getting away from the fact that it's a classic of its genre.

'Holy cow!', thinks a small cadre of SAHB fans that had previously dismissed *The Loch Ness Monster* as too chatty. 'I gotta get that!' To them, I would say hold the bus and consider this: At 38 seconds long, it takes less time to listen to 'I Love Monsters Too' than it does to read Silverton's review above. Also, phrases such as 'one of the sweetest, finest lullaby sing-alongs you've ever opened your ears to' and 'a classic of its genre' are examples of hyperbole gone mad. One can only assume 'I Love Monsters Too' was the first track Silverton heard after years of music deprivation torture during long-term captivity in North Korea.

The *Loch Ness Monster* release was attractively packaged despite being issued by the Canadian budget label K-Tel. It was housed in an appealing gatefold sleeve, with the inner side displaying a map of the loch and the locations of the sightings. Also included was a sixteen-page booklet, which took the form of Alex's diary and included photos of the interviewees. According to Stuart Cruickshank, a former BBC Radio Scotland producer interviewed by *Mojo* in 2007, between five and ten thousand copies of the album were pressed before K-Tel got a new managing director who promptly pulled the plug on the Nessie album for having low sales potential. Eddie Tobin, who had taken over managing the band following Bill Fehilly's death, then personally tried selling it to record stores and to gift shops around Loch

Ness. It received a CD release on Voiceprint in 2009, by which time the term 'audiobook' had entered the language.

How well the album succeeds depends on how much the listener believes, or wants to believe, in Nessie; what one person finds fascinating could bore another to proverbial tears. We will give the last word to Sandy Smart, another of Alex's interviewees. Asked if he could have been imagining things regarding his sighting, Smart replies, 'yeah' perhaps just a tad too hastily. A flummoxed silence follows.

Rock Drill – The Sensational Alex Harvey Band

Personnel:
Alex Harvey: vocals, guitar, trumpet
Zal Cleminson: guitars, backing vocals
Tommy Eyre: keyboards, backing vocals
Chris Glen: bass guitar, backing vocals
Ted McKenna: drums, backing vocals
Produced at Ridge Farm, Dorking, with the Maison Rouge Mobile and at Basing
Street Studios, London, by the Sensational Alex Harvey Band
Release Date: March 1978
Label: Mountain
Highest Chart Place: Did not chart
Running time: 37.13

Harvey was back by early summer 1977 and the band reconvened to work on
Rock Drill, the long-awaited follow-up to *SAHB Stories*. Unfortunately, a bust-
up between Harvey and Hugh McKenna led to McKenna walking out, leaving
SAHB flying without one of their key creative engines. Hugh's replacement
was Tommy Eyre, who had played the distinctive organ on Joe Cocker's 1968
chart-topper 'With a Little Help from My Friends', and who would become
musical director for Wham! in the 1980s.

In August, the band played their third Reading Festival, part of an eclectic bill
that included Hawkwind, Wayne County and the Electric Chairs, Racing Cars,
The Motors, and SAHB's old Knebworth best buds, the Doobie Brothers. It also
saw them reunited with their official Stateside photographer, Janet Macoska.

Alex told me if I ever came over to London, he would love to have me stay
at his house with Trudy, young son Tyro and their two golden retrievers,
Sheba and Hey You. It took me till 1977 to take him up on that offer. SAHB
headlining the Reading Festival was the magnet for me. I wanted to see and
photograph that. Alex hadn't been well. His manager and best friend had
died in a plane crash and his back had taken a beating from some of his
stage antics. I was able to photograph the band's rehearsals and show, and
pretty much anything I wanted to. Little did any of us know that Reading
would be the last time the band would play together.

Alex Harvey Jnr. talked about that final performance to the *Glasgow Herald* in
2021.

When SAHB played the Reading Festival in 1977, my dad had run out of the
strength and anger he'd channelled following the deaths of Leslie and Bill.
His management was a mess. In terms of contracts, I don't know how much
was written down and how much was just word-of-mouth. He was tangled
up in a lot of legal shit.

At Reading, I knew something was wrong. He'd run out of steam; he should have had a break. He was definitely very depressed. Today, there would have been some kind of an intervention ... he'd have received professional help.

Despite his problems, Macoska's greatest memory of Harvey at this time was his big-heartedness.

Alex was amazingly generous when I was at his house in 1977. He pulled open his phone book and started dialling up some photographer friends. He called Chalkie Davies. He said, 'Janet's here from America. I want you to invite her over and tell her everything you know'. And Chalkie did! He is still a great friend today.

It turned out, also, that Mountain Management had used a bunch of photos I had given him for private use and turned them into publicity photos. Alex told me to write an invoice for the value of that, marched me down to his management and told them to pay it and put it in cash so I could use it on my trip. Thirty minutes later, I had a lovely packet of cash for my first trip to London. Amazing.

(Note: At that time, Chalkie Davies was a staff photographer at the *NME* and shot many of the music weekly's iconic covers. He later co-founded *The Face* magazine and, with Carol Starr, shot album covers for bands including The Specials, The Pretenders, and Elvis Costello).

Meanwhile, there were tensions within SAHB. 1976 might have been ground zero, but '77 was the year punk broke, and Harvey embraced it wholeheartedly, never missing the opportunity to remind people he had predicted it. The rest of the band were less convinced, as Zal related to David Eastaugh on the *C86* podcast: 'We were accomplished musicians and when punk came along, we gave it the thumbs down. We were quite snobbish, really, saying, 'What is this? These guys can't even play well''. With this in mind, it should come as no surprise that they were having none of it when Harvey suggested they become a punk band. In *SAHB Story*, Ted remembers Alex 'wanting us to take on a new identity, which I found absurd. It was like he was saying, let's pretend not to be able to play anymore, let's regress'. In *All That Ever Mattered*, the drummer recounts Alex wanting 'me to lift all preconceptions and turn everything on its head. He was reciting a poem with ferocious lyrics and I was trying to play, trying to make sense and Alex was wanting it to not make sense, and eventually, I cracked. I picked up the kit and threw parts of it around the room and Alex went 'That's it! That's it!"

Despite these traumas and tantrums, *Rock Drill* was in the can, the band were booked to play BBC2's *Sight and Sound in Concert* series, and a major European tour loomed on the horizon. 'But' said Glen in *SAHB Story*, 'the tour was never going to happen. Alex was in no fit state to do it. He looked ill, pale, jaundiced. Even if his head was all right, his body wasn't. It would have taken a personal trainer, no drink, a special diet, steroids, weeks of preparation ...'

Four days before the tour was due to start, Alex walked into the rehearsals at Shepperton Studios and told Ted McKenna that he 'couldn't do this anymore'. Ted nodded, shook his hand, told him it had been fun, and watched him leave. After five sensational years, the band was no more.

When *Rock Drill* appeared the following February, music press ads announced it was 'The last word from the Sensational Alex Harvey Band. File under 'Genius' in your History of Rock index. You'll never hear the like again'. As it transpired, not many people heard it at all, as *Rock Drill* became the first SAHB album (with Alex) since their debut to fail to chart. Sales would have suffered because there was no tour to promote the album, but it wasn't helped by poor reviews. *The Bracknell Times* sniped that it was no pity the band had split up as 'Harvey seems to have lost a lot of the polish and power that made him one of the most exciting entertainers in the world', and advised readers to judge the band by their earlier work. Even the *NME*'s usually effusive Charles Shaar Murray dismissed much of the album as 'tedious in the extreme' and was particularly critical of Tommy Eyre's influence. *Rock Drill* did have its supporters, just not within the rock press, with *The Acton Gazette* calling it 'a varied and impressive set' and noting that 'Alex is on fine form, his vocals as gritty and compelling as ever'.

'The Rock Drill Suite Part 1: Rock Drill' (Harvey, Eyre)
Tommy Eyre gets his first SAHB songwriting credit with the first song on the album, and he opens it with an ominous keyboard piece recalling the classic Universal horror movies of the 1930s. In comes Cleminson, maintaining the mood with a scything four-chord descending scale that, were it a movie soundtrack, would signify the title monster's appearance on screen. The band switch gears just after the minute mark to introduce an up-tempo hard rock groove with an insistent stabbing organ and guitar, and Harvey's lyrics reflect his interest in both the environment and science fiction. So far, so thrilling, and not dissimilar to what Hawkwind were doing with their then-recent *Quark, Strangeness and Charm*, that is, to react to punk and new wave without pretending to be punk or new wave. Unfortunately, the third act blows it as the pace slows to glacial and henceforth, it is all plinkety-plink piano and the 'Look! I'm a musician' attitude that punk was trying to sweep aside. Adding another verse and chorus or just cutting the song short would have made it stronger.

'The Rock Drill Suite Part 2: The Dolphins' (Harvey, Cleminson, Glen, H. McKenna)
Here's Tommy Eyre on his own again but displaying a lighter touch than that used in the previous song's introduction; this is music that day could break

to. Cleminson joins in, making his guitar whistle, appropriately enough, like a dolphin. Things get marginally rockier after an introductory verse from Alex that continues the themes of 'Rock Drill', with Zal producing a short whale song-styled solo before verse two, and Eyre indulging in some Wakeman-esque noodling after. Although Hugh McKenna gets a co-credit here, his and Eyre's playing styles are noticeably different, with Tommy much more prog-orientated than his predecessor, who was more drawn towards the pop perfection of Paul McCartney.

Equally of interest is the lack of vocal restraint that Harvey displayed on *SAHB Stories*, as by verse three, which includes a lyrical nod to 'The Hammer Song' from *Framed*, he is in his fullest Gonzo Glaswegian mode to date. Whether subconsciously or not, it was clear any American dream of conquest was over.

'The Rock Drill Suite Part 3: Rock 'n' Rool' (Harvey, Cleminson, H. McKenna)

After featuring so prominently on the previous two tracks, Tommy Eyre is all but invisible here, popping up in the middle eight to lay down some ethereal synthesiser vibes. This is the calm at the centre of a song in the shape of a thunderstorm, as the SAHBs revel in their head-on collision with heavy metal. Cleminson riffs away like he has traded in his emerald harlequin suit for a red schoolboy uniform and Ted adds punchy, punk primitivism. The band were defunct by the time *Rock Drill* came out, but it is easy to imagine 'Rock 'n' Rool' becoming a live favourite given the chance.

'The Rock Drill Suite Part 4: King Kong' (Max Steiner)

It is easy to forget nearly fifty years on how audacious it seemed – how audacious it *was* – for a rock band to cover a cabaret standard like 'Delilah', especially a band like SAHB that hadn't yet landed on Mainstream Island. Three years later, the band were a lot closer to the mainstream, what with having several top twenty albums and a couple of hit singles to their name, but it transpires covering 'Delilah' was just the Looney Tune short before their audacious Main Feature, an abridged version of the score of the 1933 film classic *King Kong*.

'Max Steiner invented the Hollywood score as we know it', Harvey told Peter Silverton of *Sounds*, and he wasn't just being a fanboy bumming up his favourite movie ('I've seen the original film, I think 23 times', he proudly announced). Steiner is often given the sobriquet 'the father of film music', not only because he created original work when using pre-existing music was still the norm, but because, as Christopher Palmer explains in his book *The Composer in Hollywood* (1990), he was a pioneer that recognised the power of music to manipulate the audience's emotional reaction to what they are seeing on screen. Steiner would go on to score other iconic movies such as *Gone With the Wind* (1939), *Casablanca* (1942), and most of the Fred Astaire/ Ginger Rogers musicals.

So much for the source, but what about SAHB's interpretation of Steiner's *Kong* score? In a word, and it is a word I have deliberately avoided except where absolutely appropriate, it is sensational. Ted McKenna's primitive approach in the previous track was clearly just a warm-up for his tribal drumming here, and Tommy Eyre is so exceptional I have looked at several sources beyond the album sleeve just to ascertain there is no orchestration here. No doubt the listener's appreciation will be increased if they are a fan of the film and Steiner, but even allowing for overdubbing, there is no denying the musicianship on display here, successfully aping (Yep! I went there!) an eighty-piece orchestra to capture Steiner's towering Wagnerian motifs as well as his quieter Debussy-styled moments.

'Booids' (Traditional, arranged by Harvey, Cleminson, Glen, T. McKenna, Eyre)
As stated under the entry for 'The Man in the Jar', looking for 'Booids' using three different search engines didn't reveal the Persian tribe Harvey said they were, but instead just two possibilities, the booidea family of snakes and this, a tune by the Sensational Harvey Band. And despite being listed as 'traditional' in the songwriting credit above, this instrumental is such a natural successor to the previous track, one is inclined to believe Steiner wrote it. Perhaps, for example, for the scene where the natives prepare to sacrifice Ann Darrow to Kong?

'Who Murdered Sex?' (Harvey, Cleminson, Eyre)
After a couple of instrumentals, the SAHBs return to song. There is some vocal misdirection as Harvey performs a mini scat at the beginning, before the band launch into a raucous glam rock number, a cross between T. Rex and Mott the Hoople, with Eyre hitting the canine-worrying, high-pitched C notes that Elton John had a propensity for in his glitter years. There is even a shouty bit ('Not Me!', in answer to the title question) that has all the brattishness of the Cooper group. The spoken mid-section, however, is undeniably Alex Harvey. 'Who Murdered Sex?' is another lost concert favourite.

'Nightmare City' (Harvey)
If 'Who Murdered Sex?' gazed fondly upon the musical past, 'Nightmare City' saw the band looking tomorrow straight in the eye. They had turned their hand to no end of musical styles in their previous output, and with this urgent, driving post-punk number, they demonstrate they could keep up with the young 'uns. Here, they are reacting to punk and new wave by *being* punk and new wave, and they pull it off without sounding self-conscious or as if they are having a laugh, and at no point does 'Nightmare City' sound like pastiche. Cleminson doesn't see it that way, saying 'Nightmare City' was 'hurriedly recorded as if someone was desperate to take a holiday or book in for some lateral therapy'.

'Water Beastie' (Harvey, Glen, H. McKenna)

'The past is a foreign country', wrote L. P. Hartley in his 1953 novel *The Go-Between*, 'they do things differently there'. And here to prove his point are four whiteys from Glasgow and one from Sheffield singing in Afro-Caribbean accents, badly, and possibly inspiring 10cc to do the exact same thing later that year.

'Mrs. Blackhouse' (Harvey)

This song was a gossamer-thinly disguised attack on Mary Whitehouse (1910-2001), Britain's self-appointed campaigner for public decency, who had previously been the target of Deep Purple's 'Mary Long' and was one of the titular trio in Pink Floyd's 'Pigs (Three Different Ones)'. As if the title wasn't enough, lyrics such as 'Mrs Christian without soul' and 'Are you gonna put a ban on people kissing?' would leave British audiences in no doubt who this song was targeting.

'Mrs. Blackhouse' is itself the target for invective in online reviews, and Martin Keilty, author of *SAHB Story* and manager of the 21st-century version of SAHB, dismisses it in his book as 'a piece of crap'. This seems a bit much for what is a pleasant folky song with much strumming of acoustic guitar that could be the Strawbs, Lindisfarne, or simply a pub singalong, and a huge improvement on the preceding track. Much of this vilification seems more about what this tune is not, which is a song called 'No Complaints Department', almost certainly the 'poem with ferocious lyrics' that Ted McKenna alluded to above. 'No Complaints Department' was a highly personal piece that Alex had written that had appeared on the Norwegian and German releases of *Rock Drill*, and even on initial UK pressings, before being replaced by the offending 'Mrs. Blackhouse'. According to Jimmy Grimes, Harvey's old pal from the Soul Band days and co-author of 'No Complaints Department', it was Harvey himself that decided on the album's original closing track being withdrawn as he worried the words would upset his parents.

'Mrs. Blackhouse' was the final single release from the Sensational Alex Harvey Band, with non-album track 'Engine Room Boogie' appearing on the flipside. It is pleasant enough, but perhaps a track like 'Nightmare City' would have been more in keeping with the zeitgeist and allow the band a greater chance of going out with a bang. That said, the equally folk-tinged 'Run For Home' returned the aforementioned Lindisfarne to the charts in July 1978 after a six-year absence, so as ever predicting the record-buying public was a futile undertaking. Either way, 'Mrs. Blackhouse' flopped, it and *Rock Drill* testament to the fact that in the 1970s, touring was the most effective way of pushing your product.

Related Songs
'No Complaints Department' (Harvey, Jimmie Grimes)

'Mrs. Blackhouse' may have been the subject of some overly harsh criticism, but there is no denying the song it replaced was a much stronger piece.

We've met it before, back when it was called 'I Learned About Woman' on Harvey's solo album *The Blues*, but now Alex retitled it and gave it a fresh set of lyrics. The resulting 'No Complaints Department' is spiritually akin to John Lennon's 'God', in that they both sound like a primal scream therapy wrapped up within the structure of a song. Whereas Lennon catalogues what he no longer believes in, Harvey lists what he has lost.

'I've seen stars disappear in a hurry/Overdoses of satin and silk' references the death of Elvis Presley in August 1977, while old Soul Bandmate Robert Nimmo, a victim of recurring mental illness, was the inspiration behind the line 'They took my old pal to the madhouse'. The song's most devastating couplet opens the second verse and bluntly references the respective demises of manager Bill Fehilly and brother Les Harvey: 'So my best friend died in a plane crash/My brother was killed on the stage'.

On the first two verses of 'No Complaints Department' Harvey is accompanied only by Tommy Eyre on piano and there are also musical parallels between this and the Lennon song, both in tone and the soulful piano blues style used. The rest of the band join on the first chorus, and by the end of the session, an emotional Harvey broke down in tears. It was the last thing he recorded with SAHB.

'Engine Room Boogie' (The Sensational Alex Harvey Band)
Everyone works hard to convince the listener that the B-side of 'Mrs. Blackhouse' is exciting, but in truth, Harvey was sleepwalking his way through songs like this back in his Hamburg days. It would have sounded dated even in 1978, and the production is muddied; either it was recorded live – the band did perform it at Reading the previous year and a version did appear on a subsequent *Live at Reading* album – or it was recorded in an actual engine room. Between this and 'Satchel and The Scalphunter', SAHB were bowing out as Masters of the Underwhelming Flipside.

115

The Mafia Stole My Guitar – Alex Harvey

Personnel:
Alex Harvey: vocals, guitar,
Matthew Cang: lead guitar, keyboards, vocals
Simon Charterton: drums, percussion, vocals
Tommy Eyre: keyboards (main), vocals
Gordon Sellar: bass guitar, vocals
Don Weller: saxophone, horns on 'Oh Spartacus!'
Produced at Morgan Studios, London, by Danny Beckerman and Matthew Cang
Release Date: 1979
Label: RCA
Highest Chart Place: Did not chart
Running time: 42:23

The fallout from SAHB's dissolution wasn't pretty. Post-Alex, Mountain Records and Mountain Management put out a press release clearly intended to paint Harvey as the villain, with Cleminson press-ganged into being spokesperson. It read:

> I want Alex to know he sabotaged a great band. SAHB had just completed *Rock Drill*, which, in my opinion, is our best album to date. I was with Alex for five years, and expected a lot more loyalty than he has shown. Since he decided on the spot to retire, he has not been in touch with any of us, either to explain or apologise. You don't treat fellow members of a band this way.

In an effort to keep some sort of ball rolling, Mountain came up with Zal, AKA the Zal Band, a new outfit comprising Cleminson, Glen, Ted McKenna, and new recruits Billy Rankin and Leroi Jones. Rankin was a 17-year-old *wunderkind* guitarist and Jones a former dancer with The Tubes, now elevated, improbably, to lead singer.

After some warm-up shows in Sweden, the band embarked on an extensive college tour, starting at the Bolton Institute of Technology on 17 February. 'J. O.' of the *Sheffield Star* caught their show at the local polytechnic, concluding, 'All in all there was nothing earth-shatteringly original – just good old-fashioned rocking with enough lunacy to drive the poly wild'. The *NME*'s Andy Gill, attending the same gig, was considerably more scathing, particularly of frontman Leroi Jones: 'He consistently obscured the meaning of song after song, possibly in the belief his 'dynamic stage presence' would make up visually for what he lacked aurally. It didn't'. Most other reviews were equally unfavourable, not just of Jones but the whole band, and after just six weeks, the Zal Band called it quits. The whole venture, Cleminson admitted on a *Cat Tales* podcast (2021), was 'a bit ill-conceived'.

The end of the Zal Band marked the end of their time with Mountain, and the former members of SAHB soon found their equipment impounded and each of them presented with a bladder-relieving bill for £70,000 (approximately £556,500 in 2023) to cover their debts. Naturally, this left the band reeling and wondering how they could have had sold-out tours and top twenty albums and singles and still find themselves with considerably less than nothing to show for it.

Both their former day-to-day managers, Derek Nicol and Eddie Tobin, have weighed in in the past (see the books by Kielty and Munro) on the naivety of the band, stating that they didn't realise that they, SAHB, paid for band and road crew accommodation, the hire of sound and light equipment, the transport, the hire of rehearsal facilities, the end of the road parties, management salaries, and so on, and the £70,000 bill apiece was, presumably, a result of them spending more than the combined income generated by album, concert ticket, and merchandise sales. If one is willing to park their thinking, this seems a reasonable conclusion, but it doesn't take into account the role of management and their abject failure to manage. One does not need to be a music industry veteran to work out that the function of the musicians was to write, record, promote, and perform the music, while the function of management includes financial management, that is, ensuring income is greater than outgoings. Or perhaps that's naivety talking.

Mountain also had Harvey in their sights. He had walked out on a European tour for which sponsors were procured, venues booked, sound and lighting hired, and transport and accommodation arranged, and all these providers would be within their rights to expect Mountain to honour these deals either partially or in full. Under these circumstances, it is no surprise Mountain began legal proceedings against Harvey for breach of contract, and these were to rumble on for years. They also took out an injunction on him disposing of any equipment that belonged to the company and, significantly, an injunction on him recording or performing any new material.

Harvey had hired the London Palladium for 5 March with the intention of premiering his long-awaited *Vibrania* concept album, or so the music press said. If true, the injunction put paid to that, and the audience had to settle for SAHB songs and covers, including a waltz reading of 'Anarchy In The UK'. However, the fact that no *Vibrania* material has surfaced since suggests it was rumour and wishful thinking.

The Palladium was a British institution that had played host to the world's most celebrated performers, from Petula Clark to Josephine Baker, Bing Crosby to the Beatles (the term 'Beatlemania' was coined following their October 1963 performance there), but if Alex hoped some of the venue's past glories would rub off on him, he was to be sorely disappointed. The mononomously-named Miles was there reporting for the *NME*:

It's pretty hard to go away for a year, make a triumphal return before an audience of hard-core fans and then blow it with just one concert. But he did. He did it in style too — complete with an orchestra, dancing girls and a

Scots pipe and drum band all shuffling round stage. It was tragic. He should have cancelled the show. Instead, he almost cancelled his career.

Harvey's old Giant Moth colleague George Butler attended the show and wasn't impressed. 'The band were like a bunch of narcoleptic session musicians', he told John Neil Munro. *Melody Maker*'s Allan Jones saw things differently, writing, 'It was an extraordinary evening. Someone in the audience shouted it was good to have him back. 'Ah ain't ever bin away, bebby', he replied'.

Seemingly oblivious to any resentments his former bandmates might have, Harvey had sent them front-row tickets for the show; the singer was – hopefully – equally ignorant of the fact his management billed the ex-SAHBs for the tickets. Perhaps unsurprisingly, they did not attend. *Rock Drill* was released amidst all these shenanigans, but only the fanatical were buying. It was a record without a band, and if not quite a dead duck, it had acquired a very bad limp.

By June 1978, the lineup of Harvey's New Band had settled on teenage guitarist Matthew Cang, Simon Charterton (drums), Gordon Sellar (bass), Don Weller (saxophone), and latter-day SAHB man Tommy Eyre, stepping once more into the breach after a brief tenure from Hugh McKenna. The band toured the UK and Europe in late 1978 and began recording their debut album, *The Mafia Stole My Guitar*, the following year.

The album was released in November 1979 to overwhelmingly positive reviews. *Aberdeen Press and Journal*'s unidentified music correspondent noted that Harvey 'made some funky sounds' on the new album, and concluded that it was 'Good stuff, this. Sensational almost'. According to *Melody Maker*'s John Orme, 'Harvey's writing still has bravado, but he seems wiser and more reflective now. Another pair of songs of the calibre of 'Wait For Me Mama' and 'The Whalers' to replace the album's two oddballs, and Harvey would have had a near-faultless vindication of his former status'. Sandy Robertson of *Sounds* opined that 'Alex delivers enough on this record to make me hope that someone from the RCA office will call right off and tell me where and when I can rectify my error in never having seen him onstage'.

In the first month of the new decade, Harvey embarked on a short four-date tour to promote *The Mafia Stole My Guitar*, and RCA, emboldened by the glowing endorsements, took out ads in the music press urging the readership that it was 'your chance to see one of rock's greatest showmen'. Not many took them up on their offer. Barbara Day, writing for the *Newcastle Evening Chronicle*, reported that at the City Hall concert, 'Fans were pretty thin on the ground although they made up for the embarrassment of empty seats with their volume and enthusiasm'. After a strong start, Day reported that 'Harvey couldn't sustain the excitement, and there were plenty of lulls which degenerated into downright boredom by the end of a mammoth two hours, with people leaving early to escape the monotony'.

Confession time: On 10 January 1980, I was in the Renfield Bar in Glasgow's City Centre, just a block down from the Apollo, when someone came in offering free tickets to the Alex Harvey concert which was just about to start. It transpired that Harvey had sold just 300 tickets for a theatre with a 3,500 capacity, one that he had sold out over three consecutive nights for his triumphant Christmas shows just over four years earlier. However, my mates and I had met up for some beers and a chat and weren't in a concert frame of mind. Besides, music had undergone a seismic upheaval since SAHB's glory dates, and Harvey seemed like old news. We politely declined the tickets, which naturally is something I have regretted ever since.

'Don's Delight' (Don Weller)
Don Weller wrote this up-tempo sax-heavy soul instrumental, and it sounds purpose-built for any '80s TV show Mike Post was unavailable to score. It also sounds like the perfect number to fanfare Harvey on stage, but surprisingly cropped up mid-way through the main set.

'Back in the Depot' (Harvey, Matthew Cang)
Matthew Cang's guitar replaces Weller's sax as the prominent instrument, but the intro is still very much in telly soundtrack territory, with Cang to the fore with a cheesy prime-time solo. The song soon settles down to allow Harvey to croon the first half of the opening verse, but before the song is out, he will have amped up the Glaswegian further than he ever did with SAHB, taking it dangerously close to self-parody. In an artistic flourish best described as 'curious', he then mimics Charley, the cartoon cat who warned kids about various dangers in public safety ads on British television in the 1970s (non-British readers: type 'Charley Says' into YouTube and see what I'm gibbering about). Whatever his idiosyncratic singing styles, there is still power in Harvey's pipes, his vocal delivery at odds with reports of health issues and poor performances that regularly cropped up in the music press.

'Back in the Depot' hasn't got a particularly strong melody, and when Cang reprises his opening solo in the mid-section, it now sounds like a cry in an aural wilderness. If the track works at all, it is because Harvey has once again surrounded himself with some top players, with Don Weller's sax and Simon Charterton's drumming imbuing a dynamism that the song never fully earns.

'Wait For Me Mama' (Harvey, Weller, Cang, H. McKenna)
Hugh McKenna returns to lend songwriting support but does not play on this or his other co-writer credit, 'The Whalers (Thar She Blows)'. Whether due to McKenna's presence or not, 'Wait For Me Mama' is a marked improvement on the previous track.

With a title like that, one would be forgiven for expecting some blues or early rock and roll, but Harvey says 'head east, young band' instead, and that's just what they do, with Charterton laying down some tribal beats and someone, presumably Weller, playing what sounds very much like a pungi, the instrument traditionally used to charm snakes.

Things are kept to a minimum until the first chorus, after which the song builds until it becomes a Very Big Production Number. The middle eight could be the score for a film like *She* (1965), or indeed any other H. Rider Haggard 'white guys in a lost African city' adventure. Harvey did like such 'Boy's Own' stories.

'The Mafia Stole My Guitar' (Harvey)
So far, Tommy Eyre (keyboards) and Gordon Sellar (bass) have gone unmentioned, but they both stamp their mark on the title track, the album's first out-and-out hard rocker. The song begins with Eyre laying down some washes, which Cang overlays with some distorted guitar howls before letting loose the album's first big guitar riff. As has been the case in the two previous songs, the instruments fall away somewhat to allow space for Harvey's voice, but Sellar's bass remains omnipresent, powering the song with its mean and moody pulse. Cang contributes a pleasing featherlight solo in the middle section, by which point even those missing the old gang had to admit these new boys were really rather good.

Harvey sings of the Mafia stealing 'the old time Telecaster' and he is, of course, referring to the theft of an instrument he had owned since his pre-Hamburg days, along with all of SAHB's other gear, in Miami in 1975. 'In the old Cuba woods, they was selling my goods', he bemoans, before punningly beseeching, 'Oh, godfather, why has thou forsaken me?'

Harvey's work post-SAHB is often overlooked, but *The Mafia Stole My Guitar* is shaping up nicely, and the title track is a late-career classic.

'Shakin' All Over' (Johnny Kidd)
The trend of taking an old song and 'punking it up' was a feature of punk from day one, as the inclusion of Chris Montez's 'Let's Dance' on *The Ramones* and the Damned's placing 'Help' on the flip of 'New Rose' demonstrates. Although no one would mistake Harvey and his New Band for punks, here they decide to give Johnny Kidd and The Pirates' 1960 chart topper the same treatment, and in doing so, produce a track with two very different halves.

Things start off well, with frenetic guitars, keys and sax replacing the original's distinctive raunchy, percussive rhythm guitar masquerading as bass. So far, so good, even if Harvey's vocals are too low in the mix and he is singing them not so much in speeded-up punk style but more as if he is in a hurry to be somewhere else.

The wheels come off this particular bus mid-section with a keyboard solo that cries prog, and when the third verse begins, the band play in the style of the original, as if forgetting their stated mission of zapping the song with a punkover. No matter, here's Alex to keep it punk, but one suspects a sherry refreshment has been enjoyed during the musical interlude, and the Harv keeps it punk by laying down the single worst vocal track of his lengthy career. Someone, and all eyes are on producer Danny Beckerman, should have paraphrased Larry Olivier in discussion with Dustin Hoffman on the set of *Marathon Man*: Have you tried singing, dear boy?

It was nearly 100 pages ago, but those wanting an Alex Harvey cover of 'Shakin' All Over' that is good are redirected to the version he recorded on the Soul Band's unreleased second album.

'The Whalers (Thar She Blows)' (Harvey, Cang, H. McKenna)

Knowing Harvey's deeply felt concern for the animals we share our planet with, it is a safe bet to assume that 'The Whalers (Thar She Blows)' is not the romanticised sea shanty suggested by the title, even if the opening lyric hints in that direction: 'Gimme the spear, gimme it quick/And I'll kill the son of Moby Dick'. Instead, the song is a raging polemic against the consumer whose need, through ignorance or indifference, leads to the wholesale killing of our fellow creatures – 'Slaughter cubs and mummy too/Here's a perfume just for you' – with Harvey reserving a special circle in Hell for those that decry the whaling industry but don't change their purchasing habits accordingly: 'You can't complain, it's fair enough/We kill it and you buy the stuff'.

Musically, the song starts as a ballad with some light jazzy piano and drum flourishes, lovely lone piano accompaniment on the midsection, and then blasts into some aggressive funk with wailing saxes and synthesised whale song for the final third.

It's all going rather well, but then thar he blows it. Harvey has developed a habit of going off the rails with his vocals in the final third of every song on this album, and 'The Whalers' is no exception. On one hand, band (including Alex) and producer are changing tempos to keep long songs interesting, but on the other, Alex brings an irritating commonality to all songs by over-egging that Glasgow accent. In the review of 'Back In The Depot' above, I stated that Harvey was sailing dangerously close to caricature, but here he is well and truly stranded on Parody Island.

'Oh Spartacus!' (Harvey, Cang)

Some more animal sound effects, this time Don Weller using brass to mimic the trumpet of an elephant, and some more tribal tubthumping from Charterton open the album's penultimate track. Cang occupies the ears next, first with a dirty riff followed by some soloing that suggests he has just discovered 'Jessica' by the Allman Brothers, and then Harvey starts singing in a voice that suggests he has been listening to Alex Harvey, but only the one that sang on this album. None of which prevents 'Oh Spartacus' from being a filthy little groover with some great sax in the middle eight.

'Just a Gigolo/I Ain't Got Nobody' (Irving Caeser, Julius Brammer, Leonello Casucci/Roger A. Graham, Spencer Williams)

By taking two standards from the early twentieth century and combining them into a melody in 1956, Louis Prima not only revitalised his flagging career but created an entirely new standard. Here, the New Harvey Band perform a straightforward reading of Prima's arrangement, and Alex manages to keep his vocals in check.

Related Songs
'Wake Up Davis (Sings the Oil Man Boogie)' (Harvey)
This flipside to the 'Shakin' All Over' 45 starts with slow twangy blues guitar before launching into the big, bold, and brassy retro rock and roll that Roy Wood was so fond of, and there is even a hook that subconsciously urges one to remember that they are a Womble. Despite the glam edges, this sounds like something older, something that might have been kicking around since the Hamburg days. If new at the time, then it is an uncanny reconstruction of what the Soul Band were pumping out nearly two decades earlier.

'Big Tree (Small Axe)' (Bob Marley)
Some pulsing synths explode into a big '80s pop fanfare before devolving into cod reggae of the Coconut Airways variety – synthesised steel drums, anyone? However, the strong arrangement makes up for that small misstep, and 'Small Axe', as the original Bob Marley song was titled, was a perfect choice for Harvey, since he too had railed against the big tree that was the record industry. Unfortunately, he never sounds as if he is taking the track seriously, and by delivering a vocal that matches his 'Shakin' All Over' in sheer awfulness, he renders the song unlistenable. Incredibly, this was released as a single in 1980.

The Soldier On the Wall – Alex Harvey

Personnel:
Alex Harvey: vocals
Tony Lambert: keyboards
George Hall: keyboards
Ian 'Toose' Taylor: guitar
Jack Dawe: bass guitar
Colin Griffin: drums
Andy Nolan: percussion
Gordon Sellers: bass on 'The Poet and I'
Tommy Eyre: keyboards on 'The Poet and I'
Ray Conn: harmony on 'The Poet and I'
Produced at Kingsway Recorders, Holborn, London, by Alex Harvey and Kevin D. Nixon. 'The Poet and I' produced by Ray Conn.
Release Date: 1982
Label: Powerstation Records
Highest Chart Place: Did not chart
Running time: 40:32

The 1980s got off to a disappointing start for Harvey with the poorly attended UK shows mentioned above, but what was happening with his erstwhile colleagues from his most successful band?

Faced with a crippling bill from Mountain and with no musical opportunities on the horizon, Cleminson took the pragmatic route and found himself a 'proper' job as a taxi driver. This he did for a year or so and, incredibly for a city the size of London, one of his fares was his old boss. 'One day I went round to make a pick-up', he told *Mojo* (2000), 'and by sheer coincidence, it was Alex and his new guitar player Matthew (Cang). I said, 'Fucking hell, Alex! How are you? Get in!' Cleminson points out that Harvey was in no way judgemental of his former six-stringer's new occupation. 'Great, you've got yourself a gig', he said. 'We'll all get by'.

Later, Harvey got in touch with Zal with a view to reforming SAHB, but Cleminson declined, unconvinced by the new songs Harvey played him. As it turns out, Harvey's offer wasn't the only one Zal received. Pete Agnew, bass player with Nazareth, takes up the story in the sleeve notes for the 2010 reissue of *No Mean City*:

About halfway through working on that album, it was suggested we get Zal Cleminson into the band. It was our manager Derek Nichol's idea, because Mountain Management managed the Alex Harvey Band. They'd split up and disappeared to the four corners of the earth, and at one point, Derek told us that Zal was driving a cab. He was one of the best guitarists we had ever seen and it was hard to believe. We all loved Zal so when Derek suggested that he come and join Nazareth, we all went, 'Sure! Let's do it'.

As well as adding greater intricacy to the guitar sound, Cleminson contributed the track 'Simple Solution (Parts 1&2)' to the album, which was named for the 1930s novel by McArthur and Long. He also wrote or co-wrote all the songs bar one on the follow-up long player *Malice In Wonderland*.

Chris Glen played with headliner John Martyn at Glastonbury in 1979 and then had a very busy 1981, guesting on Cozy Powell's all-star *Tilt* album and then joining the Michael Schenker Group for their second long player, *MSG*. Powell was behind the kit on that album and the next, the live *One Night at Budokan*, but when he departed to join Whitesnake his drum stool was occupied by none other than Ted McKenna, thus reuniting the SAHB rhythm section. Ted's first Schenker Group album, *Assault Attack*, also featured another Harvey Band alumnus, Tommy Eyre.

McKenna had been quick to find a new gig following SAHB's dissolution, replacing the wonderfully named Rod de'Ath as Rory Gallagher's sticksman. Ted first appeared on *Photo-Finish*, which arrived in stores in October 1978, just six months after SAHB's swan song, as well as *Top Priority* (1979) and the live *Stage Struck* in 1980. He continued touring with Gallagher for a couple of years and appeared on Greg Lake's self-titled debut (1981).

Many, including his bandmates, considered Hugh McKenna to be the most musically gifted of SAHB, but he was also its biggest casualty. During his argument with Harvey that led to him walking out, McKenna had angrily reminded Alex that his commitment to the band resulted in two 'mental breakdowns'. This was no hyperbole as Hugh was indeed struggling with his mental health, a situation that was exacerbated by his dependency on drugs and alcohol. Hugh disappeared into the shadows far beyond the sodium glare to confront his demons, but actually defeating them was a process that would take many years.

Meanwhile, it was time for Alex Harvey to face his final curtain. His new band had died of neglect and the old trooper had rounded up a posse of Welsh musicians he dubbed The Electric Cowboys. In late 1981 they entered the studio to work on a new album *The Soldier On The Wall*, and in early 1982 they played some European dates to preview the new songs. Their gig in Vienna on 25 January is available on YouTube, but it makes for painful viewing. Harvey spends much of the time looking sometimes disinterested, sometimes confused, as if he has forgotten why he is there. He often stands by the amps at the back of the stage, and on several occasions, someone standing behind the amps – a tour manager? a roadie? – is clearly pleading with Harvey to get back up front and sing the next song. At one point, this individual can be seen consulting with Harvey before lying his head face down on the amp in utter defeat. All too often, Harvey leaves his poor band stranded, and they have to produce lengthy improvisational pieces to cover for their errant frontman; guitarist Ian Taylor is constantly looking over his shoulder with the bewildered look of someone clearly wondering what the fuck is going on, and bassist Jack Dawe gamely smiles and bounces nimbly up and down, as if to convince the audience both he and they are having a good time. The performance improves somewhat when songs from the new album are played, but *The Soldier On The Wall* is a long way from being released and these new tunes are totally unknown to the audience.

It was while coming home from this tour that Alex Harvey had a heart attack. He was standing on the quayside in Zeebrugge, Belgium, awaiting the ferry, when he suddenly clutched his chest. 'This is it, boys', he reportedly gasped before collapsing. The ferry was held up to see if Alex would recover, but it soon became clear he required hospitalisation. Halfway across the channel, the Electric Cowboys received the terrible news; Alex was dead, having suffered a second heart attack *en route* to hospital. It was 4 February, the day before his 47th birthday.

Soldier On The Wall would languish until November 1983 before finally securing a release two years after it was recorded. *Uncut*, reviewing the CD reissue a decade later, gave it 1 ½ stars out of five without ever saying why. In his Harvey biography, Munro concluded that 'Even the most charitable of fans would have to agree that on the evidence of this album, Alex's days as a relevant and influential artist were long gone' and states the album is 'marred by some poor production and sloppy, repetitive songs'. *Allmusic's* retrospective review is kinder, plumping for a four-star rating and calling it 'one of Harvey's most fulfilling albums ever'.

'Mitzi' (Harvey)

The church organ sound that briefly opens 'Mitzi' can throw the listener off track with its timeless nature, but the thunderous drumming and heavy synths that follow leave no doubt: Alex Harvey has entered the 1980s. Having said that, this straightforward pop song sounds like it could have been recorded by the Tremeloes or Dave Dee and company many years earlier, making it appear very much a Sixties song in Eighties clothing.

Of interest is the lack of an exaggerated accent. Having adopted it a decade previously, did Alex recognise that its time was over and that a new decade called for a new approach? We will never know, but this new approach was certainly welcome after the vocal histrionics on *The Mafia Stole My Guitar*.

'Billy Bolero' (Harvey)

In a Tex-Mex tale that could have been lifted from the Westerns Alex enjoyed as a child, the titular character has hung up his guns and seeks a quiet life, especially when he comes across Maria dancing in her velvet gown. 'She looked across the room to where he stood', the lyric tells us, 'and they fell in love as only lovers could'. Not everyone is happy with this situation, not when Maria was betrothed to another, so her father 'took his shotgun down/ And he put poor Billy in the ground'.

The song benefits from changing tempos and some evocative Mariachi brass that, while sadly uncredited, compliments the lyrics perfectly. Harvey is on form, delivering a strong world-weary vocal. 'Billy Bolero' might not embrace the Eighties as enthusiastically as the preceding track or the revisiting of 'Roman Wall Blues' below, but it demonstrates that while his latter-day live appearances could be shambolic, Harvey was still capable of knocking out a decent tune in the studio.

'Snowshoes Thompson' (Paul Mason Howard, Buddy Ebsen)

After colonising what is now the United States of America, white Europeans found themselves in a land low on myths and legends (those of the native people didn't count, of course, as that would have meant acknowledging them), so they set about creating new ones. Thus, we have Casey Jones, famous for crashing a train, and John Albert Thompson, AKA Snowshoes Thompson, famous for delivering the mail. None of these sound particularly awe-inspiring, but in Thompson's defence, his mail route took him over the treacherous Sierra Nevada mountain range, and he regularly undertook the five-day round trip when most of us would have called it a snow day. It is perhaps for this reason that ol' Snowshoes has not one but two songs in his honour, the first a 1952 single by Tennessee Ernie Ford and the second a 1960 album track by Johnny Horton.

It is the former that Harvey and company tackle here, and they deliver a rambunctious but otherwise faithful rendition. This is traditional Grand Ole Opry stuff, complete with yee-hahs and accordion, and whereas 'Mitzi' evoked the Sixties but sounded fresh, 'Snowshoes Thompson' sounds exactly like a song that is three decades old and sticks out like the proverbial sore thumb.

Worryingly, Harvey reprises his 'Charley Says' vocal from *The Mafia Stole My Guitar*, but it is mercifully brief.

'Roman Wall Blues' (Harvey, WH Auden)

The rapid martial drumming and descending synths that open this track announce that this is very much a widescreen adaptation of the title track of Harvey's 1969 solo album, with big '80s production values replacing the guitar-led psychedelic blues of the original. The changes leave the song much improved as the former late-night small club number is transformed into the score of some onscreen epic (Michael Mann's 1992 *The Last of the Mohicans* springs immediately to mind). As with that particular soundtrack, there are strong Celtic underpinnings here, no more so than in the coda, which would align this rousing version of 'Roman Wall Blues' with contemporaneous releases by U2, Big Country, and, most surprisingly, SAHB's old touring pals Slade.

The two-man percussion team of Colin Griffin (drums) and Andy Nolan (percussion) have been terrific thus far, but here they bump up to stellar.

There are a million Alex Harvey compilations out there, none of which contain this version of 'Roman Wall Blues', and that is a real shame as it deserves a wider audience.

'The Poet and I' (Frank Mills, Ray Conn)

Produced and co-written by long-time friend Ray Conn, this is very much in the traditional Scottish folk music genre and wouldn't feel out of place in the repertoire of musicians such as the Corries and Alastair McDonald. It starts as a piano ballad before building into something altogether livelier, and the poet in question is Robert Burns, with several of his works – Tam O' Shanter, Highland Mary, A Red Red Rose – namechecked in the lyrics.

It was released as a single in November 1983 under the amended title 'The Poet and I (If I Could Write Like Robbie Burns)' with a 'singalong version' on the B-side. Quite who it was aimed at is impossible to discern, but with the charts cluttered with Culture Club, Duran Duran, Howard Jones and the like, it was always going to be a no-hoper. This is the album's second sore thumb.

'Nervous' (Harvey)

Another song, another style, this time a hard rocker in the AC/DC mould, with Harvey even approximating a Brian Johnson vocal in places and guitarist Ian Taylor cutting loose on a blistering solo. Full of riffs and hooks, 'Nervous' puts the album back on track.

'Carry the Water' (Harvey, Tony Lambert, Ian Taylor, Jack Dawe, Colin Griffin)

Seven songs in and the album is onto its fifth, maybe even sixth genre. 'Carry the Water' is a bluesy gospel piece with some honky-tonk keys and choir-style backing vocals; less obvious inclusions are the fat crunching guitar chords and a short spell of yodelling. Harvey's vocals have been fine throughout *The Soldier On The Wall*, but here he is definitely the weakest link. There is no denying his exuberance, but his clarity is shot. One again suspects liquid refreshments.

'Flowers Mr. Florist' (T. Powell)

'What this album needs' thought someone or other, 'is yet another music genre', so here's some doo-wop, courtesy of this cover of the Ink Spots' 1953 song 'Flowers Mr. Florist'. The eclecticism displayed here makes SAHB sound like Status Quo, but this 'something for everyone' approach dilutes the record as a whole, and with no singular identity, it begs the question: who was *The Soldier on the Wall* for?

'The Poet and I (Reprise)' (Mills, Conn)

It does what it says in the title by reprising track five for a pointless minute and a half.

Posthumous Releases

There is a bewildering number of Alex Harvey compilations on the market now, some focusing on the Soul Band years, others spotlighting only his sensational Seventies outfit, still others his solo work, and finally others that present a career-wide retrospectives. This chapter provides a brief guide to the best of the bunch.

The Last Of The Teenage Idols (Universal, 2016)
This fourteen-disc box set is, without a shadow of a doubt, the best Alex Harvey collection available. Unfortunately for anyone seeking it out now, it was only released as a limited edition and is, therefore, both scarce and pricey. At the time of writing, no copies were being offered on eBay, but some were available on discogs.com, starting at around the £300 mark.

That is a big financial commitment, but what you get is the (almost) complete Alex Harvey. The eight SAHB albums are there in their entirety, and each come with bonus material, including non-album B-sides, live recordings, BBC sessions, and the spoken word US promo disc *Alex Harvey Talks About Everything*. Also included is much of Harvey's pre-SAHB work, such as the first Soul Band record and *The Blues* album with just Alex and Les Harvey on guitars, but the compilers of this box have gone the extra mile and included the second, unreleased Soul Band disc and *The Joker is Wild* oddity from 1972. Best of all, though, is his work with Giant Moth, the Hairband, and Rock Workshop.

Neither of his two post-SAHB albums are presented in their entirety, but five choice cuts from each will give listeners a rough insight into *The Mafia Stole My Guitar* and *The Soldier On The Wall*. Four tracks from the *Alex Harvey Presents The Loch Ness Monster* project are thrown in for good measure.

The discs come with a lavishly illustrated hardback book featuring family snaps courtesy of Trudy Harvey, a wide cross-section of photographs of Alex and SAHB by Janet Macoska and illuminating prose by Tim Barr. All this comes housed in a sturdy slipcase with front cover art courtesy of future SAHB frontman Max Maxwell.

Less pricey but equally difficult to find is the 4 CD version of the box, which obviously comes with a much-truncated number of tracks. An average of four songs culled from the SAHB albums (although the least of those albums *The Penthouse Tapes* is afforded eight of the original ten), and there is a much-edited representation of the pre-and post-SAHB years. Barr's sleeve notes and the photo selection are also proportionately less than in the parent set.

Considering the Situation (Universal, 2003)
When Universal acquired the rights to the Harvey back catalogue, they reissued the seven SAHB studio albums and *Live* as four twin packs in 2002.

The following year they released their first Harvey retrospective, *Considering the Situation*, a two-disc, 37-track affair, with the first focusing on the Soul Band, a couple of *Hair* songs and a handful of solo numbers, and the second dedicated to SAHB. It is a smaller but more available and affordable alternative to the two *Teenage Idols* sets.

Shout: The Essential Alex Harvey (Spectrum/Universal, 2018)
This 3 CD, 54-track set is the ideal option for those dipping their toes into Harvey waters for the first time. All but thirteen of the tracks are a comprehensive best of SAHB, with nine Soul Band numbers and four solo songs. The Soul Band songs comprise tracks from both the 1964 *Alex Harvey And His Soul Band* album and its unreleased follow-up. To paraphrase Joe Friday in *Dragnet*, this collection features just the songs, ma'am, with no liner notes or credits, and is available at this time of writing via various online retailers for about six bucks.

Alex Harvey Teenage A Go Go (Alchemy Entertainment, 2003)
According to the cover, it took ten years to put this release together, so it would have been nice if some of that time was spent writing decent sleeve notes. What is known is that the nineteen tracks span Harvey's 'earlier work from his Soulband (*sic*) days up to 1968' and that they were taken from acetates found amongst the possessions of Alex's one-time manager David Firmstone. Beyond that, the sleeve notes practically revel in their vagueness. We are told 'it's *probably* the Hairband on this track (Big Louis)', that another ('Dance of the Green Scarab') features 'maybe noseflutes or an oboe – who knows?' or, a personal favourite this, 'I'm not 100% convinced that this is Alex'. There are also no songwriting credits, which one could rightly expect of a disc that took ten weeks to compile let alone ten years.

That aside, this is a fascinating release, albeit one for the Harvey completist only. Only three of its nineteen tracks appear on the *Teenage Idols* box, and two of them – 'Going Down To Birmingham' and 'Jailhouse Rock' – are culled from the rare *Everything is Allright With Isabella Bond* album; the third is 'The Blind Man' from the first Soul Band record. Worthy tracks include a cover of Dylan's 'The Wicked Messenger' and 'Told You Twice Already', which sounds very much as if it had been inspired by early Lennon-McCartney songs.

Of note is 'The Ballad of John F. Kennedy', a Woody Guthrie-styled folk song written by Harvey and Jimmy Grimes that points the finger squarely at the Ku Klux Klan and accepts that Lee Harvey Oswald was exactly what he said he was, a patsy. This rarity is also available on a rather unusual album called *The Ballad of JFK: A Musical History of the John F. Kennedy Assassination (1963-1968)* from Light In The Attic. This gathers twenty pieces of music recorded in the five years following Kennedy's murder, including three separate tracks called 'The Ballad of John F. Kennedy'.

The album's standout song by some distance is a reading of Blake's 'Jerusalem', apparently recorded circa 1968 for an unreleased choral album curated by Harvey's then-manager David Firmstone. Harvey starts softly, almost hesitantly, his vocal just heard above the accompanying Brighton Festival Choir, but he soon finds his voice and strides off like a colossus across England's mountains green. Alex sings the song with reverence and this track alone makes *Teenage A Go Go* worth seeking out.

Balanced against this is 'Man: A Space Hymn', which sounds like Joe Meek on a bad day, and a rendition of 'My Grandfather's Clock', which according to the sleeve notes 'comes from a children's record series where there were nursery rhymes set to music'. What this record series was and who else was involved in it goes unrecorded.

Live At The BBC (Spectrum/Universal, 2009)

As the title suggests, this two-disc set collects all the band's recordings for the BBC. Disc one is compiled from two radio sessions taped at the Beeb's Paris Theatre. The first was recorded in November 1972, and showcases five numbers from their debut album *Framed* and a barnstorming cover of Sly and The Family Stone's 'Dance To The Music', then a regular in the SAHB setlist. For the second Paris Theatre show, in October 1973, the band delivered five tracks from their then-newly released Next album.

Disc two contains recordings of SAHB's *Old Grey Whistle Test* appearances, meaning that there are doublers of both 'Next' and 'The Faith Healer', as well as a July '76 *Top of the Pops* rendition of 'Boston Tea Party'. The set is rounded off with 'Pick It Up and Kick It' and 'Smouldering', the two tracks SAHB (Without Alex) performed on *OGWT*, an especially welcome inclusion since *Fourplay* has long been out of print on CD.

Hot City: The 1974 Unreleased Album (Major League Productions, 2009)

Finally, we have *Hot City*, billed as unreleased but really the abandoned Shel Tarmy-produced first attempt at what eventually became *The Impossible Dream*. This is really for completists that want to contrast the difference between the two recordings only.

The *Hot City* 'Vambo' has a less heroic chorus than the finished article, wherein 'Vambo rules, okay' rather than coming to our rescue. The mix is also a bit bass-heavy, giving new definition to the word 'throbbing'. 'Man In The Jar' has a slightly different intro, with Hugh counterbalancing Zal, Chris, and Ted's heavy funk with some light-fingered jazz. The biggest change, however, is Harvey's vocal, where he sings like he has a prior engagement. Listening to it puts one in mind of those credits on 1980s TV shows that scrolled too quickly for the viewer to read.

Alex sings 'Hey You' on the *Hot City* original, even managing a convincing Chris Glen impersonation on the opening line before returning to his more familiar growl, while 'Long Haired Music' has a slight metal edge with Cleminson's riffing more to the fore.

There are two significant differences between the *Hot City* and *The Impossible Dream* versions of 'Anthem'. The first is the deployment of the pipes during the introduction of the song on the *Hot City* take, a sterling example of too much, too soon. David Batchelor makes the right call on *The Impossible Dream*; by reserving the pipes for the coda, he allows the song to build organically throughout, whereas Shel Talmy's start-stop-start approach risks robbing the song of, well, its anthemic quality. The second change is the title, as 'Anthem' was called 'Last Train' at the time of the Talmy sessions.

The final major change is the inclusion of 'Ace In The Hole' from the *Hot City* sessions. This song was not retained for *The Impossible Dream*, possibly because it was too close to 'Hey' and 'Sergeant Fury' in evoking the pre-rock and roll era.

The label behind *Hot City*, Major League Productions, also released two worthwhile live SAHB albums, *British Tour 76* (2004) and *US Tour 74* (2006). The latter is notable for its sixteen-minute version of 'Anthem' and the complete 'Hot City Symphony'. Both are worthwhile with decent production, although *Live* or *Live At The BBC* would be the recommended first stops for concert documents.

Last Ride of the Sensational Alex Harvey Band

Hugh spent much of the 1980s side-lined by his personal demons, but the rest of the SAHB boys kept busy. Both Chris and Ted continued with Michael Schenker up to and including 1984's *Rock Will Never Die*, although both would return to the Schenker fold later.

After growing disillusioned with Nazareth, Cleminson formed the short-lived supergroup Tandoori Cassette with ex-Jethro Tull drummer Barriemore Barlow, Charlie Tumahai of Be-Bop Deluxe, and Ronnie Leahy, who had been in Stone the Crows before becoming an in-demand session musician. They only recorded one single, 'Angel Talk/Third World Briefcase', which demonstrated that these Seventies stalwarts were ready for the Eighties. The A-side was in the vein of emerging bands such as Talk Talk and the Psychedelic Furs, while the flipside anticipated mid-Eighties acts such as Red Box and Latin Quarter. Unfortunately, the single was never released.

Chris also found himself in a short-lived supergroup of sorts, GMT, with Robin McCauley of Grand Prix and Phil Taylor of Motorhead. They released one self-titled EP in 1986 to deafening indifference. And not to be outdone, Ted too got in on the supergroup act, being one of the rotating players, along with the likes of Brian May, Glenn Hughes, John Wetton and Don Airey, that played on albums by prog outfit Phenomena.

By the end of the decade, Zal had been treading the boards with Bonnie Tyler, Elkie Brooks, and Midge Ure, and Chris and Glen had reunited as part of Ian Gillan's eponymous band, and in the 1990s, Ted would spend some time playing for Womack & Womack. It was while with them he came up with an idea he called the Sensational Party Boys.

The basic concept was this: to form a core band that big names could hook up with when they were in town. Chris was immediately interested and Zal took to the idea once he realised no touring was involved. The band played at the Rock'n Horse in the Cathcart area of Glasgow, and amongst those that lent their vocals to the project were Dan McCafferty, Maggie Bell, and Fish. Hugh resisted the call, but eventually agreed to step in when Ronnie Leahy couldn't make a show and just like that, the Sensational Party Boys decided to call a spade a spade and the Sensational Alex Harvey Band were reborn. It didn't last long, but it did result in a CD called *Live In Glasgow 1993*, which featured a selection of SAHB favourites and, bizarrely, a cover of the Michael Schenker Group's 'Armed & Ready', an odd choice considering it predates Chris and Ted's time with MSG. Handling the vocals was Stevie Doherty of Glasgow band, Zero Zero.

In April 2002, the full SAHB line-up reconvened at Glasgow's Cava Studio to record a track for a Frankie Miller tribute album. It was the first time they had been together in six years, not that one could tell from their excellent rendition of Miller's 'Dancing In The Rain'. The Marmalade's Dean Ford provided lead vocals. SAHB also played on Fish's version of 'Caledonia', the

McKenna cousins appeared on Lulu's reading of 'It's As Good As Gone', and Hugh plays keyboards on Miller Anderson's cover of 'In My Own Crazy Way'.

That September, the band took part in a concert celebrating Miller at the Barrowlands. Their set consisted of 'The Faith Healer', 'Delilah', and 'Boston Tea Party' with Billy Rankin front and centre, while Ford took charge of the microphone for 'Dancing In The Rain'. The highlight of the show, in the humble opinion of this scribbler at least, was a magnificent version of Marmalade's 'Reflections Of My Life'.

Their appearance at the Miller tribute inevitably led to talk of getting back together. Some sporadic concerts within Scotland took place in 2003, with a summer show in Glasgow's celebrated King Tut's Wah Wah Hut, followed by a mini festive tour taking in Aberdeen, Kilmarnock, and, bizarrely, the Grand Ole Opry in Glasgow, which is normally every bit as 'ride 'em, cowboy' as the name suggests.

Billy Rankin bowed out in early 2004, and his place was taken by Max Maxwell, a more flamboyant performer who wisely didn't try to ape Alex but brought his own sense of showmanship to the role. By the following year, Cleminson had worked out how to present his old mime face in a new way, thus increasing the theatricality of the band and making them more recognisably SAHB, but the guitarist didn't want to stop at just reinventing his face paint. Concerned that SAHB was in danger of becoming its own tribute act, Zal set about rearranging some of their old favourites in an attempt to make them sound fresh and new, and this led to some tension within the band. Glen puts forward the case for leaving things alone in *SAHB Story*:

> If you're calling yourself SAHB and you're asking people for ticket money... guess what the audience wants? They want to hear the original versions of the songs, in the spirit they remember them. We changed 'St. Anthony' so much that Max couldn't work out how to sing it.

While admitting that not all his changes had been the correct call, Cleminson was adamant it was the right thing to do:

> I'm not sure which is worse: an unwillingness to express something new and different in the true spirit of a progressive rock band; or feeling overwhelmed by the mere idea of it. I don't enjoy being lazy and I don't like repeating myself.

Despite the dissension within the ranks, audience response to the shows was universally positive, so the band ploughed on, organising a 22-date UK tour that would take them from Southampton to Kirkwall. A CD souvenir of the tour was released in 2006 called *Zalvation: Live in the 21st Century,* and it inadvertently exemplifies the old vs new debate. The long, slow-building introduction to 'Vambo', for example, would have left fans puzzled as to what was coming next, and things wouldn't get any clearer once the no longer familiar riff kicked in. It is only at the chorus that the identity of the song becomes unmistakable. On 'The Faith Healer', there is no attempt to replicate the Tootal Bug drone, Hugh McKenna instead laying down a series of dreamy keyboard washes before Zal's guitar unleashes a metal ferocity unheard of in the original.

These new arrangements make for an interesting and satisfying CD listening experience for the veteran SAHB fan who will already have the traditional reading of 'Vambo' on *The Impossible Dream*, *Live*, *US Tour 74*, *British Tour 76*, and possibly even *Live in Glasgow 1993*. When it comes to the concertgoer, however, Glen is correct to assume they expect familiarity. One only needs to look upon the sea of baffled faces at any given Bob Dylan concert over the past two decades, and hear that murmur fill the auditorium after someone recognises what is being played and the word spreads. A possible solution to the dilemma might have been to release a studio version of the reworked songs prior to touring them, but that would have led to a new level of costs and risk.

2006 saw the band's two biggest dates in terms of audience, when on 10 June, they played the Sweden Rock Festival on a bill that included Chris and Ted's old employer Michael Schenker, not to mention heavyweights like Alice Cooper and Whitesnake. A week later, they were at the Hallam FM Arena in Sheffield supporting Def Leppard and Cheap Trick, both of whom included massive SAHB fans amongst their members.

2007 saw the band's 21st-century success continue to grow as they toured Europe and Australia, but by the time the year was ending, Cleminson knew it was time for him to leave. 'In truth, we could never really progress without Alex, or indeed his collaboration with Hugh', he said in *SAHB Story*. 'It would be impossible for me to turn SAHB into anything meaningful, as I don't have a suitable repertoire of original musical ideas'. The band briefly soldiered on, drafting in guitarist Julian Hutson-Saxby, but the beast had been mortally wounded and would expire early in 2008.

While playing with the revived SAHB, Ted McKenna worked as a lecturer in applied arts at North Glasgow College, a post he held until 2011. He left to join Rory Gallagher's long-time bassist Gerry McAvoy in his Band of Friends project, a group dedicated to keeping alive the Irish guitarist's music. He appeared on two of their albums, *Too Much is Not Enough* (2013) and *Repeat After Me* (2016) and won the 'Best Musician (Performance)' Award at the European Blues Festival for his work with them.

In 2017, both he and Chris Glen reunited with Michael Schenker for a Japanese concert featuring all three vocalists that had served in MSG, Gary Barden, Graham Bonnett, and Robin McAuley. The success of this gig, dubbed Michael Schenker Fest (MSF), led to a four-date UK tour, which was later released on CD and vinyl. He and Glen both featured on the subsequent studio album *Resurrection* (2018).

Ted McKenna died suddenly on 19 January 2019 of a haemorrhage during a routine hernia operation. He was 68. Owen Mullen wrote his friend's eulogy, which included this description of McKenna's dedication to his craft:

> A roadie from the old days contacted me when he heard the sad news and reached into the distant past, the late 1960s, for his abiding memory of the guy whose drums he had set up at Airdrie Town Hall, the Trocadero in Hamilton, and hundreds of other gigs across Scotland. He said, 'Do you remember how Ted drove us all mad with his practice pads?' I had to smile. I started my final conversation with Ted by asking what he was up to. 'Just got the practice pads out', was his reply.

After the 21st-century incarnation of SAHB dissolved, Hugh McKenna lived quietly with his wife in London. His only forays into the studio included a self-released album by Paul Meehan in 2009 (*The Gods Have Forgotten Us*) and one track on the MSF album *Resurrection*. He passed away after a short illness on 18 December 2019. 'The last time I spoke to Hugh', said Mullen, 'I asked him what he did all day. 'I feed the cats', he said. That's not how it should have ended. Zal was fab and Ted was a great drummer, but Hugh was really the musical heart of SAHB'.

Chris Glen returned to touring with Michael Schenker for a couple of years from 2008, and, as mentioned, returned to the MSF reiteration of the band in 2017, appearing on the *Resurrection* album and its 2019 follow-up *Revelation*. He also joined the reformed version of 1970s Edinburgh proggers Café Jacques, playing on their 2011 mini-album *Lifer*, and formed his own band, Chris Glen and The Outfit. They have released three online tracks at the time of writing, and play a mix of classic SAHB, MSG, and original material at their gigs. They play primarily in Scotland's central belt. He released his autobiography, *The Bass Business*, in 2017.

When Zal Cleminson left SAHB, he also left the music industry for nearly a decade. He came out of retirement in 2017 and, joining forces with tribute act The Sensational Alex Harvey Experience, formed a new band called Zal Cleminson's sin'dogs. They released an EP in 2017 and an album, *Vol. 1*, the following year, and the sound reflected a return to the hard rock of Tear Gas but filtered through various later musical genres, such as heavy metal, grunge, and industrial metal. Cleminson's sin'dogs played small venues across Britain, but in 2019 they also supported Mott the Hoople at the Glasgow Barrowlands, played Fairport Convention's Cropredy Festival and made their European debut at the Sweden Rock Festival. Cleminson left the band later that year to form Orphans of the Ash with former sin'dog Billy McGonagle. Their first album *Ellipsis* was released in November 2022.

As with Glen and the McKenna cousins, Cleminson's greatest legacy will always be his years in the Sensational Alex Harvey Band and the music they made. I asked him if he could summarise the band and his time with it:

The way it ended was somewhat inevitable but still a saddening experience. Our accolades were bittersweet; there was little to show, financially, for the level of commitment and adoration the band enjoyed. The music was equally ambivalent, often brilliant and sometimes unique and at times self-indulgent and rather pointless. My fondest memories will be of the camaraderie, the professionalism and the sheer energy of playing live to the best and most loyal fans, I prefer to call friends.

Alex Harvey may have been gone, but he was not forgotten. He didn't live on in song, sadly, as disappointingly few artists covered his material. 'The Faith Healer' comes out best, with versions by Helloween, Saxon, and The Cult, among others; both Britny Fox and the Dead Daisies gave 'Midnight Moses' a go; and Fish tried out 'Boston Tea Party' on his 1993 covers album *Songs From The Mirror*. The great coverer of songs was not a great coveree, but Robert Smith, Joe Elliot, and Bobby Gillespie were among those that gave spoken endorsements.

However, by the turn of the new millennium, his name started cropping up more frequently. There he was being featured in *Mojo* and *Record Collector* or cropping up on a BBC Radio Scotland documentary which soon begat a televised version. Along came the books, John Neil Munro's *The Sensational Alex Harvey* coinciding with the twentieth anniversary of Harvey's passing, and Martin Kielty's *SAHB Story* heralding the risen band. That phoenix-like return at the Frankie Miller concert and subsequent tours was surely manna to the faithful, and going by the ever-increasing venue capacities, the band were also making some new converts as well.

After a three-decade snooze, Glasgow suddenly remembered the man Glasgow newspapers often called the city's favourite son. On the thirtieth anniversary of his death, a tree was planted in Harvey's memory in the grounds of the People's Palace Museum and a commemorative bench installed in the museum's Winter Gardens. As well as a plaque with Harvey's birth and death dates, it has the legends 'Last of the Teenage Idols' and 'Let Me Put My Hands On You' inscribed in the top of the backrest. An exhibition was also held with stage clothes, memorabilia, and a selection of Janet Macoska's photographs of Alex and the band. A year later, the bench was joined by a small bust of Harvey by Ayrshire sculptor Sandy Campbell, who captured well the grin, to use Charles Shaar Murray's memorable expression, 'that hit his face like an earthquake'. The £1,000 bust was commissioned by fan Stuart Donaghey, who was able to raise the money via donations from Harvey fans across the world. 'I know he would not believe he would end up with a bronze statue in the People's Palace', Alex Jnr. said at the unveiling.

Later that year, on 29 November, a terrible accident occurred. A police helicopter crashed into a pub in Glasgow city centre, the Clutha, resulting in the deaths of all onboard the aircraft and seven of the pub's patrons.

Thirty-one people were injured. The Clutha eventually reopened in July 2015 in a ceremony attended by First Minister Nicola Sturgeon, but while it was undergoing repairs, a stunning black and white mural depicting some of its illustrious clientele was created to commemorate the pub. The mural included Stan Laurel, Benny Lynch, Spike Milligan, Frank Zappa, Billy Connolly, Jimmy Reid. And Alex Harvey, standing there in his stripey top, arms folded across his chest. Gallus. Subways in his teeth. Vambo rules.

In 2018, the National Museum of Scotland in Edinburgh hosted an exhibition called *Rip It Up: The Story of Scottish Pop*. It goes without saying that SAHB were among the featured artists, with Ted and Zal appearing in the promotional video where various homegrown musicians try to sum up Scottish pop in three words or less.

So, Alex and the band maintained a presence on the pop culture landscape in many ways, but as the 2020s rolled around, things changed. The exhibitions at both the National Museum and at the People's Palace had been and gone. So, too, had the mural, which progressively deteriorated at the hands of vandals and the elements until being replaced entirely in 2020. The previous year, the People's Palace and Winter Gardens closed, having been found to be structurally unsafe. The People's Palace reopened after a £350,000 refurbishment in June 2019, but Glasgow City Council, which owns the building, say they don't have the £5m+ required to restore the Winter Gardens, which as of spring 2023 remains closed. All the plants have long been rehoused, so the Harvey bench presumably sits in there gathering dust. The Harvey bust was moved to the Queen's Park Glasshouse for reasons obscure, but it too has been closed with no sign of ever reopening. Hopefully, someone at Glasgow City Council will get a grip and rehouse both bench and bust in the People's Palace.

Only three of the eight SAHB albums released in the band's lifetime are available on Amazon, *Tomorrow Belongs To Me* and the 'two-for' containing *Framed* and *Next*. They are all CDs; none of the band's work has been re-released on vinyl. The three MLP releases are available (*Hot City*, *US Tour 74*, and *British Tour 76*), but these are aimed at the dedicated fan rather than the casual browser. There are a number of compilations, but not many options available to those who want to investigate further. Surprisingly both the released and unreleased Soul Band albums are available in both CD and vinyl format, but don't come cheap. A quick look in my local Fopp and HMV reveals an even greater paucity of product.

The mural, the bust, and the bench might be permanent losses, but thankfully the situation with the albums being out of print is not the kiss of death it once was. We live in a digital age, a world undreamt of when these records were made, the world of Spotify, Amazon Music, YouTube, and their ilk, where everything is available all of the time. Even when those titans are gone, and go they inevitably will, they will have successors who will themselves have successors, all of whom have the power to preserve the music of the Sensational Alex Harvey Band, the Soul Band, Harvey solo, and Tear Gas, possibly forever. Here's hoping they're up to the task.

In the meantime, they are all there. *Next. The Impossible Dream. SAHB Stories.* All the rest. They are an invitation, and to reply all you need do is click the button.

Are you going to the party?

Bibliography

Blair, E. (2012, 5 September). The Strange Story of the Man Behind 'Strange Fruit'. NPR (*National Public Radio*)

Brown, M. (1977, 24 February). The Monsters in Alex Harvey. *Rolling Stone No. 233.*

Burnside, A. (2012, 29 January). Sensational: Thirty years after his death, Alex Harvey's music is still influential. *The Scotsman.*

Clayson, A. (1997). *Hamburg: Cradle of British Rock.* Sanctuary Publishing, London.

Davenport, R. (2016, 20 April). 'Keeping the Faith'. *Record Collector* 453

Day, B. (1980, 12 Saturday). Sensation turns to monotony. *Newcastle Evening Chronicle.*

Deller, F. (2007). 'Time Machine: Alex Harvey Dies, 4 February 1982'. *Mojo* Issue 149, February 2007.

Doherty, M. (1976, 7 August). Harvey's History Lesson. *Melody Maker*

Gibson, D. (1957, 28 April). 'He is Scotland's, Tommy Steele! Back street kid wins stardom chance'. *The Sunday Mail.*

Glasgow Evening Times. (2019, 18 July). Greatest Glaswegian: Curators of words and sounds... in running to be city's greatest. *Evening Times.*

Glen, C. & Keilty, M. (2017). The Bass Business. Noisewave

Heller, J. (2018). *Strange Stars: David Bowie, Pop Music, and the Decade Sci-Fi Exploded.* Melville House, Brooklyn.

Jones, A. (2018) *Can't Stand Up For Falling Down.* Bloomsbury, London.

Keilty, M. (2013). *SAHB Story: The Tale of the Sensational Alex Harvey Band.* Noisewave Publishing

Leadbetter, R. (2016, 12 March). 'From Gorbals to Greatness: Alex Harvey by his widow Trudy'. *Glasgow Herald.*

Leadbetter, R. (1995). *You Don't Have To Be In Harlem: The Story of the Most Celebrated Rock Venue in Britain.* Mainstream Publishing, Edinburgh.

McNair, J (2000). Let's All Drink to the Death of a Clown. *Mojo* Issue 77, April 2000

Morrison, R. (2021, 28 February). Robbie Morrison on 1930s Glasgow: The gangs and the Tartan Untouchables. *The Herald.*

Munro, J. N. (2002). *The Sensational Alex Harvey.* Fire Fly Publishing, London

Murray, C. S. (1974, 12 October), *The Sensational Alex Harvey Band: The Impossible Dream, New Musical Express*

Northam, R. (1974, 5 October). Alex Harvey Band ... at the Town Hall, Birmingham. *Birmingham Daily Post.*

Palmer, C. (1990). *The Composer in Hollywood.* Marion Boyers Publishers, London

Reynolds, S. (2016). *Shock and Awe: Glam Rock and Its Legacy.* Faber & Faber, London.

Seafield, L. (2022). *Scottish Witches.* Waverley Books, Glasgow.

Sloan, B. (2021, 7 March). Alex Harvey – The Mafia Stole My Guitar: Scotland's

Favourite Albums by Billy Sloan. The Herald, Glasgow.
Tobin, E & Keilty, M. (2010). *Are Ye Dancin'?* Waverley Books, Glasgow
Turner, G.E. & Goldner, O (2018). *The Making of King Kong*, Pulp Hero Press.
Wilson, N. (2017, 29 March). Lost Glasgow: 1930s Glasgow was cinema city glamour. *Evening Times.*

Sleeve Notes
Barr, T. (2016). Book accompanying *The Last of the Teenage Idols* Box Set released by Universal.
McIver, J. (2010). Reissue of *No Mean City* by Nazareth released by Salvo.

Websites
www.rocksbackpages.com
www.billyrankine.com
www.heraldscotland.com
www.itspsychedelicbaby.com
www.procolharum.com
www.rockingscots.com
www.rockpasta.com
www.scotbeat.wordpress.com
www.thecollegecrowddigsme.com
www.theglasgowstory.com
scotbeat.wordpress.com

On Track series
Allman Brothers Band – Andrew Wild 978-1-78952-252-5
Tori Amos – Lisa Torem 978-1-78952-142-9
Aphex Twin – Beau Waddell 978-1-78952-267-9
Asia – Peter Braidis 978-1-78952-099-6
Badfinger – Robert Day-Webb 978-1-878952-176-4
Barclay James Harvest – Keith and Monica Domone 978-1-78952-067-5
Beck – Arthur Lizie 978-1-78952-258-7
The Beatles – Andrew Wild 978-1-78952-009-5
The Beatles Solo 1969-1980 – Andrew Wild 978-1-78952-030-9
Blue Oyster Cult – Jacob Holm-Lupo 978-1-78952-007-1
Blur – Matt Bishop 978-178952-164-1
Marc Bolan and T.Rex – Peter Gallagher 978-1-78952-124-5
Kate Bush – Bill Thomas 978-1-78952-097-2
Camel – Hamish Kuzminski 978-1-78952-040-8
Captain Beefheart – Opher Goodwin 978-1-78952-235-8
Caravan – Andy Boot 978-1-78952-127-6
Cardiacs – Eric Benac 978-1-78952-131-3
Nick Cave and The Bad Seeds – Dominic Sanderson 978-1-78952-240-2
Eric Clapton Solo – Andrew Wild 978-1-78952-141-2
The Clash – Nick Assirati 978-1-78952-077-4
Elvis Costello and The Attractions – Georg Purvis 978-1-78952-129-0
Crosby, Stills and Nash – Andrew Wild 978-1-78952-039-2
Creedence Clearwater Revival – Tony Thompson 978-178952-237-2
The Damned – Morgan Brown 978-1-78952-136-8
Deep Purple and Rainbow 1968-79 – Steve Pilkington 978-1-78952-002-6
Dire Straits – Andrew Wild 978-1-78952-044-6
The Doors – Tony Thompson 978-1-78952-137-5
Dream Theater – Jordan Blum 978-1-78952-050-7
Eagles – John Van der Kiste 978-1-78952-260-0
Earth, Wind and Fire – Bud Wilkins 978-1-78952-272-3
Electric Light Orchestra – Barry Delve 978-1-78952-152-8
Emerson Lake and Palmer – Mike Goode 978-1-78952-000-2
Fairport Convention – Kevan Furbank 978-1-78952-051-4
Peter Gabriel – Graeme Scarfe 978-1-78952-138-2
Genesis – Stuart MacFarlane 978-1-78952-005-7
Gentle Giant – Gary Steel 978-1-78952-058-3
Gong – Kevan Furbank 978-1-78952-082-8
Green Day – William E. Spevack 978-1-78952-261-7
Hall and Oates – Ian Abrahams 978-1-78952-167-2
Hawkwind – Duncan Harris 978-1-78952-052-1
Peter Hammill – Richard Rees Jones 978-1-78952-163-4
Roy Harper – Opher Goodwin 978-1-78952-130-6
Jimi Hendrix – Emma Stott 978-1-78952-175-7
The Hollies – Andrew Darlington 978-1-78952-159-7
Horslips – Richard James 978-1-78952-263-1
The Human League and The Sheffield Scene –
Andrew Darlington 978-1-78952-186-3
The Incredible String Band – Tim Moon 978-1-78952-107-8
Iron Maiden – Steve Pilkington 978-1-78952-061-3
Joe Jackson – Richard James 978-1-78952-189-4
Jefferson Airplane – Richard Butterworth 978-1-78952-143-6
Jethro Tull – Jordan Blum 978-1-78952-016-3
Elton John in the 1970s – Peter Kearns 978-1-78952-034-7
Billy Joel – Lisa Torem 978-1-78952-183-2
Judas Priest – John Tucker 978-1-78952-018-7
Kansas – Kevin Cummings 978-1-78952-057-6
The Kinks – Martin Hutchinson 978-1-78952-172-6
Korn – Matt Karpe 978-1-78952-153-5

Fleetwood Mac in the 1980s – Don Klees 978-178952-254-9
Focus in the 1970s – Stephen Lambe 978-1-78952-079-8
Free and Bad Company in the 1970s – John Van der Kiste 978-1-78952-178-8
Genesis in the 1970s – Bill Thomas 978178952-146-7
George Harrison in the 1970s – Eoghan Lyng 978-1-78952-174-0
Kiss in the 1970s – Peter Gallagher 978-1-78952-246-4
Manfred Mann's Earth Band in the 1970s – John Van der Kiste 978178952-243-3
Marillion in the 1980s – Nathaniel Webb 978-1-78952-065-1
Van Morrison in the 1970s – Peter Childs - 978-1-78952-241-9
Mott the Hoople and Ian Hunter in the 1970s –
John Van der Kiste 978-1-78-952-162-7
Pink Floyd In The 1970s – Georg Purvis 978-1-78952-072-9
Suzi Quatro in the 1970s – Darren Johnson 978-1-78952-236-5
Queen in the 1970s – James Griffiths 978-1-78952-265-5
Roxy Music in the 1970s – Dave Thompson 978-1-78952-180-1
Slade in the 1970s – Darren Johnson 978-1-78952-268-6
Status Quo in the 1980s – Greg Harper 978-1-78952-244-0
Tangerine Dream in the 1970s – Stephen Palmer 978-1-78952-161-0
The Sweet in the 1970s – Darren Johnson 978-1-78952-139-9
Uriah Heep in the 1970s – Steve Pilkington 978-1-78952-103-0
Van der Graaf Generator in the 1970s – Steve Pilkington 978-1-78952-245-7
Rick Wakeman in the 1970s – Geoffrey Feakes 978-1-78952-264-8
Yes in the 1980s – Stephen Lambe with David Watkinson 978-1-78952-125-2

On Screen series
Carry On... – Stephen Lambe 978-1-78952-004-0
David Cronenberg – Patrick Chapman 978-1-78952-071-2
Doctor Who: The David Tennant Years – Jamie Hailstone 978-1-78952-066-8
James Bond – Andrew Wild 978-1-78952-010-1
Monty Python – Steve Pilkington 978-1-78952-047-7
Seinfeld Seasons 1 to 5 – Stephen Lambe 978-1-78952-012-5

Other Books
1967: A Year In Psychedelic Rock 978-1-78952-155-9
1970: A Year In Rock – John Van der Kiste 978-1-78952-147-4
1973: The Golden Year of Progressive Rock 978-1-78952-165-8
Babysitting A Band On The Rocks – G.D. Praetorius 978-1-78952-106-1
Eric Clapton Sessions – Andrew Wild 978-1-78952-177-1
Derek Taylor: For Your Radioactive Children –
Andrew Darlington 978-1-78952-038-5
The Golden Road: The Recording History of The Grateful Dead – John Kilbride 978-1-78952-156-6
Iggy and The Stooges On Stage 1967-1974 – Per Nilsen 978-1-78952-101-6
Jon Anderson and the Warriors – the road to Yes –
David Watkinson 978-1-78952-059-0
Magic: The David Paton Story – David Paton 978-1-78952-266-2
Misty: The Music of Johnny Mathis – Jakob Baekgaard 978-1-78952-247-1
Nu Metal: A Definitive Guide – Matt Karpe 978-1-78952-063-7
Tommy Bolin: In and Out of Deep Purple – Laura Shenton 978-1-78952-070-5
Maximum Darkness – Deke Leonard 978-1-78952-048-4
The Twang Dynasty – Deke Leonard 978-1-78952-049-1

and many more to come!

Would you like to write for Sonicbond Publishing?

At Sonicbond Publishing we are always on the look-out for authors, particularly for our two main series:

On Track. Mixing fact with in depth analysis, the On Track series examines the work of a particular musical artist or group. All genres are considered from easy listening and jazz to 60s soul to 90s pop, via rock and metal.

On Screen. This series looks at the world of film and television. Subjects considered include directors, actors and writers, as well as entire television and film series. As with the On Track series, we balance fact with analysis.

While professional writing experience would, of course, be an advantage the most important qualification is to have real enthusiasm and knowledge of your subject. First-time authors are welcomed, but the ability to write well in English is essential.

Sonicbond Publishing has distribution throughout Europe and North America, and all books are also published in E-book form. Authors will be paid a royalty based on sales of their book.

Further details are available from www.sonicbondpublishing.co.uk. To contact us, complete the contact form there or
email info@sonicbondpublishing.co.uk